To an Unknown Lady

To an Unknown Lady

by ANDRÉ MAUROIS

Translated from the French
by JOHN BUCHANAN-BROWN

E. P. DUTTON & CO., INC. · NEW YORK

1957

Gen'l

Published in England under the title of
To the Fair Unknown

Contents

To an Unknown Lady

You are both real and imaginary. When a friend asked me to write to you, once a week, it amused me to picture you in my mind's eye. I created you, perfect alike in your beauty and your good sense. I had no doubt that you would take on living shape from my imagination, would read my letters, answer them and tell me all those things an author likes to hear.

From the very first I gave you very definite form, that of an exceptionally beautiful young woman I had seen at the theater: not on the stage but in the audience. None of my party knew you, and yet you had lips, a voice, a body; while you remained, as was proper, the Unknown Lady.

Some of the letters were published, and I had answers from you, as I expected. I use "you" collectively in this instance. You were all women, one naive, another aggressive, a third mocking and humorous. I was tempted to open a correspondence with you but I held back. If you were to be all, you could not be one.

You reproach me for my reserve and for keeping to my design of sentimental moralizing, but what can I do? The most patient of men can only be faithful to his unknown if she makes herself known. Mérimée found out that his was called Jenny Dacquin and was soon allowed to kiss her feet, and hers were very beautiful. An idol must have feet and the rest, otherwise one soon wearies of a goddess in the abstract.

9

I promised to play this game only as long as it amused me. After sixty weeks my request for a fresh theme was granted. In the world of the imagination it is easy to break off an affair, and there is nothing to blemish my memory of you. *Adieu.*

A. M.

A Meeting

        I was with a party at the Théâtre Français the other night. "It was only Molière," but the play was very well done. Queen Soraya of Persia was laughing, Robert Kemp seemed satisfied, and Paul Léautaud drew interested stares. I heard a lady near us tell her husband, "I must telephone Aunt Clémence to say I've seen Léautaud; that will please her."

You were sitting in front of me swathed in your white fox furs; as if you had stepped from de Musset's pages, "your dark head" was poised "on a slim seductive throat." During the intermission, you leaned toward your friend, and I heard you ask her: "How can I make him love me?" I wanted in my turn to lean forward and quote the remark of one of Molière's contemporaries for your benefit: "If we would please others, we should only speak on their favorite topics, on things that are of concern to them, avoiding arguments on things indifferent, rarely questioning and never giving them grounds to think that we are more intelligent than they."

Such was the advice of a man who knew his fellow men. Yes, if we want to make someone love us, we must talk, not about what interests us but about what interests him. And what is that precisely?

Why, the person in question. We shall never bore a woman by analyzing her character or her attractions, by asking her about her childhood or about what she likes or what she wishes she had done. You will never bore a man by making him talk about himself. How many triumphs women have had in their careers as listeners, moreover they need not listen; as long as they appear to be doing so.

"Avoiding arguments on things indifferent:" if your argument is unfolded in a quarrelsome tone, it merely serves to exasperate your opponent and all the more so if you are right. "All good argument offends," as Stendhal said. Your opponent may have to admit that your reasoning is unassailable, but he will never forgive you for it. In love men seek peace not war. Happy the gentle, tender women, for they are loved the most. Nothing irritates a man more than an aggressive woman. Amazons get more admiration than adoration.

Another, very legitimate method of gaining popularity is to speak well of people. If they are told what you said, you will have made them happy and hence they will tend to think what a nice person you are.

"I don't like Madame de ....." said he.

"What a pity: she thinks you're awfully attractive and tells everyone so."

"Really? I must have misjudged her."

The reverse is also true. A malicious remark, reported with equal malice, makes terrible enemies. "If everybody knew what everybody said about everybody, nobody would speak to anybody." Unfortunately, sooner or later everybody does know what everybody says about everybody.

To return to La Rochefoucauld: "Never give them grounds to think that you are more intelligent than they." Yet surely you can love someone you admire? Doubtless, provided that his superiority is not arrogantly assumed and provided that in compensation he has some little weakness which enables the other, in his turn, to adopt a protective attitude toward him. Paul Valéry, the cleverest man I ever knew, carried his wisdom lightly. His weightiest thoughts were uttered as jokes, and his air of a naughty schoolboy made him lovable. In the same way another great mind, who is by nature more serious, amuses his friends by his unconscious pride, by his absent-mindedness and by his fads. You pardon his genius when you laugh at him, and your beauty will be pardoned because of your good nature. A woman will never bore a great man by reminding him that he is a man.

How can you make people like you? By giving those whom you wish to attract grounds for self-content. "Love begins with the mingling of one stream of happiness and well-being with another." To please is to give and to receive. There, my soul's unknown (as the Spaniards say) is the answer I wanted to give you. I will add one final word of advice, that of Mérimée to *his* unknown: "Never speak ill of yourself. Your friends will always do plenty of that for you." *Adieu.*

The Bounds of Love

Paul Valéry's remarks on love, as on all subjects, were excellent, and he liked to discuss the passions in the language of mathematics, judging, and rightly so, that the contrast between the linguistic precision of the one and the emotional vagueness of the other produced a stimulating discord. I particularly savored one of his formulas which I christened Valéry's theorem: "The quantity of love to be expressed and felt in one day is limited."

In other words no human being can possibly live for a whole day, still less for whole weeks or years on the level of passionate love. One gets tired of everything, even of being loved. It is useful to state this truth, since many young people, and old ones too, seem to be in ignorance of it. There are women who have been overwhelmed by the first heat of an affair; they have loved to hear, from morning to night, that they are lovely, witty, glorious to possess, divine to listen to while they re-echo these praises and affirm in return that their partner is the most virile of men, the cleverest, the best lover, the most delightful company in the world. All of which is infinitely pleasant, but the resources of the language are not themselves infinite. "To start with," said Robert Louis Stevenson, "conversation between lovers is easy, I am I, you are you, and no one else matters."

14

There are a hundred ways of saying "I am I, you are you." There are not a hundred thousand and the days are long and many.

"How do you describe a union in which a man contents himself with one woman?" the examiner asked an American college girl.

"Monotony!" she replied.

To prevent monogamy becoming monotony, care must be taken to ring the changes on love and the way in which it is expressed with a variety of quite different things. A married couple should regularly take the air of social contacts, common interest in work, their friends, entertainment. A compliment is only effective if it arises as if by chance, from a marriage of ideas or from a pleasure shared. It bores if it becomes automatic.

Octave Mirbeau once wrote a short story, in dialogue, of two lovers who met every night in a park by moonlight. The sentimental male murmured in tones more moonstruck even than the night: "Look . . . the bench, our dear bench!" The exasperated girl sighed: "That bench again!" Keep us from benches as places of sentimental pilgrimage. Tender phrases invented as they are spoken are charming: love expressed in formulas is irritating.

An aggressive, critical woman quickly wearies a man; a woman who accepts everything with the same naive admiration is not certain to keep her hold on him for long. A contradiction? Of course, man is nothing but contradictions. Flux and reflux. "Condemned," says Voltaire, "to pass from convulsive anxiety to lethargy and boredom." Too many human beings are so made that being loved easily becomes a habit, and they prize lightly feelings for themselves of which they are too sure.

15

A woman is uncertain of the feelings of a man toward her: she concentrates on him. Suddenly she discovers that he admires her. At first she is thankful for it, but if he tells her day in and day out that she is the sole wonder of the world, she may become bored. Another man who is less enslaved will rouse her curiosity. I knew a girl who was always ready to sing in public and whom everyone praised to the skies because she was so pretty. One young man alone kept quiet.

At last she asked him: "Don't you like my song?"

"Oh yes!" said he, "if you had any sort of voice it would be excellent."

He was the man she married. *Adieu.*

Human Nature Never Changes

I have been to the theater again; you, alas, were not there. I was sorry, for my own sake, and for yours too. I wanted to shout: "Bravo, Roussin, this is real comedy!" One scene, among others, amused the audience. A young man has made his father's secretary pregnant. He hasn't got a job; she is an outstandingly competent young lady who earns a very good living. He offers to marry her; she refuses, and as a result the young man's mother complains: "My poor boy . . . abandoned by his seducer . . . she compromised him and now she won't put things right!"

16

The reverse of the classic predicament. But that is because today the economic status of the sexes is so frequently reversed. Women are better able to earn their living than they were in the past; they are less the slaves of the whims and wishes of men. In Balzac's day a husband was a solution; in Roussin's he is a problem. Philippe Hériat's *L'Immaculée* has already shown us the girl who asks science to give her the means of having a baby without the baby having a father.

But while science is still unable to satisfy such an exclusive mother, biologists are engaged in strange and dangerous research. In his book, *Brave New World*, Aldous Huxley sets himself to describe procreation a hundred years hence. In the brave new world children are never naturally conceived. A surgical operation removes the woman's ovaries and these, stored in a suitable place, go on producing ovules which are fertilized by artificial insemination. One ovary alone is able to give sixteen thousand brothers and sisters in batches of ninety-six identical twins.

Love? Feeling? Romance? The directors of the brave new world treat such nonsense with the greatest scorn. They pity unfortunate twentieth century man, with father, mother, husband, lover. It isn't so odd, say these men of the future, that man in the past should have been mad, bad and wretched. Conflicts and complexes grew from the family, the passions and from sexual rivalry. He was forced to experience things to the full and fully experiencing them, how could he have been stable? Community. Identity. Stability is the triple motto of this loveless world.

But it is only a story and mankind, fortunately, is not taking that path. Human nature changes far less than one thinks. On the surface it may be as turbulent as the sea. Yet dive and reach down to the depths and you will be surprised to find how little the basic emotions change.

What does the youth of today sing? A song by Prévert and Kosma whose sense is "Little girl, if you think your youth will last forever, you're making a big mistake . . ." Where do they get the theme? From a four-hundred-year-old poem, Ronsard's "Pluck, pluck the bloom of your youth, for age will wither your beauty like this flower."

You could take all the themes of the poets of the Pléiade or even of de Musset and refashion them as cynical love songs for Saint-Germain-des-Prés. Do it for yourself, it's an easy, amusing and profitable game. Unknown *de mi alma*, you must make up your mind. The proud secretary in Roussin's play ends up by marrying her victim and you yourself are just like your sixteenth century sister. *Adieu.*

When Coquetry Is Necessary

"Calumny," says a character in the *Barber of Seville*, "Sir, you scarce know what you scorn." I often want to tell a woman who is too artlessly sincere in her love: "Coquetry, Madame, you know not what you despise." Coquetry remains a weapon of surprising and redoubtable power. It is the trick, so clearly noted by Marivaux, of first offering then refusing, or pretending

18

to give and then of taking back. The results of the game are unbelievable. In vain you know each move, you are still caught every time.

Yet, if you think about it, it is only natural. Without coquetry at first, to give birth to the first hope, love in most men would never be roused. "To love is to be disturbed by the idea of a possibility which turns into a craving, an overriding desire and an obsession." As long as attracting some man (or woman) seems quite impossible, we never give it a thought, any more than you are upset at not being Queen of England. All the men find Greta Garbo and Michèle Morgan wonderfully beautiful, and they admire them, but it never enters their heads to be unhappy because of them. To their legions of admirers they are no more than images on a screen; they are not possibilities.

But from the moment when a look, a smile, a word or a gesture assumes the air of a promise, our imagination, in spite of ourselves, carries the affair one stage further. This woman has given me a reason, small though it be, for hoping. From then on I am in a quandary and I ask myself: "Does she really care for me? Could she be in love with me? No, that's silly. But still, these advances . . ." In short, as Stendhal says, we "crystallize" upon her, that is to say, we dress her in our dreams, just as, in the mines at Salzburg, the crystals of salt add glitter to any object exposed there.

Little by little desire becomes obsession. A coquette who wants to make this obsession last, and enslave a man, has only to turn to a trick as old as mankind itself; to run away, after letting it be known that she wants to be chased; to refuse, at the same time leaving some grounds for hope, "Tomorrow, perhaps, I shall be yours." That is quite enough to send men to the ends of the earth for you.

You can only blame the coquette for this trick if she uses it to keep a number of her pursuers in suspense, for then she must be unfaithful and deceiving, unless she is possessed of an infinite tact and knows how to save the pride of the men to whom she grants nothing. But even the most lovable of the species runs the risk of simply exhausting all patience in the long run. She ends up, like Moliere's *Célimène* by starting so many hares that she never catches one.

Since in these soft bonds, you are quite unable to see all in me as I see all in you, Go, I refuse you. My love is outraged and I free myself forever from your unworthy chains.

On the other hand coquetry may be quite innocent, and even necessary to keep the man you love. In this case woman has no real wish at heart to be coquettish. "Love's greatest miracle is the cure of coquetry." A woman who is really in love wants to give herself unfeignedly and unreservedly, with a sublime generosity. But she may nevertheless be forced to make the man she loves suffer a little, because he is one of those who cannot live without suffering or be faithful where he is certain.

A woman sincerely in love should then feign coquetry to keep her lover's heart, just as a nurse must sometimes be pitiless to save life. An injection hurts, but it is useful. Jealousy is painful, but it keeps one faithful. If the Unknown Lady should ever reveal herself, don't let her be a coquette. I should be caught like anyone else. *Adieu.*

Mrs. Know-All

"Oh, Doctor, you're sitting next to me?"

"Yes, I on one side of you."

"I am so glad, Doctor; it's simply ages since I last had the chance of a quiet chat with you."

"I'm glad, too . . ."

"I've a thousand things to ask you: it won't bore you, will it?"

"Well, to be perfectly frank . . ."

"First there's my insomnia, you remember my insomnia? But what's this? You shouldn't take soup, Doctor!"

"And why not?"

"But you're mad. There's nothing so unhealthy as this torrent of liquid at the beginning of a meal."

"Good heavens, my dear lady . . ."

"Don't take any consommé, please, Doctor, and let's both have a look at the menu. . . . Salmon, yes. Let me see; we'll get Vitamin A in butter; Vitamin C in fruit. . . . But no Vitamin B, that *is* a nuisance: don't you think so?"

"I'll make the best of a bad job."

"Tell me, how many calories a day does a woman need who leads an active life like me?"

"I don't know exactly, but it's not very important."

"What? Not very important! You might as well say that coal is unimportant to engines or gas to cars. I live

the same sort of life as a man and I must have three
thousand calories a day or I'd die."

"You count them, I suppose?"

"Of course I count them . . . You're joking, Doctor?
I always carry my little list (She opens her handbag)
Just a moment . . . here we are. Ham: 875 calories a
pound; Chicken: 750. Milk: 350 . . ."

"Admirable; but do you know the weight of this
chicken wing?"

"At home I always have all portions weighed, but
here, in someone's else's house I have to judge as best I
can." (She gives a little scream,) "Oh! Doctor!"

"What's the matter?"

"Please . . . stop . . . you're setting my teeth on edge."

"But what have I done?"

"Doctor, you're mixing proteins and carbohydrates...
Doctor . . . please, stop!"

"Dammit! I'm only eating what's put in front of me."

"You! A great physician! But you must know as well
as I do that what the average Frenchman eats, beefsteak
and fried potatoes, is the most deadly poison in the
world?"

"But the average Frenchman survives!"

"Doctor, you're a heretic, I won't speak to you again."
(Lowering her voice,) "Who is that sitting on my
right? I've heard his name but I don't know him."

"He's an official in the Ministry of Finance."

"Not really? But how fascinating!" (She turns sharp-
ly to her right.) "And what about the budget? Have
you balanced it at last?"

"Please excuse me, I've been discussing the budget
for eight solid hours and I counted on this dinner party
for a rest."

22

"A rest. . . . We'll give you a rest when you've straightened out our affairs. . . . And it could be done so simply."

"So simply?"

"Childishly simply. . . . You have a budget of four thousand millions?"

"Yes, about that."

"Very well . . . you just reduce your expenditure 20 per cent."

(The doctor and the financier exchanged a look of complicity and despair behind Mrs. Know-All's back).

My dear, you have the wisdom of knowing nothing. That is why you understand everything. *Adieu.*

Fashion

The Comédie Française brings me luck for I saw you there again. You were one of the bevy of beauties in the dress circle, wearing a most becoming green and white gown. I could see that it was in the height of fashion. Don't think, though, that I blame you for that. Very much the reverse. My master, Alain, as great a philosopher as he was a poet, praised fashion when he said, "The first rule of dress is to reassure the wearer."

Men, and still more women, need to feel that they are at one with their surroundings. It doesn't matter to me whether I wear a lounge suit or a dinner jacket, but if I arrived at a party in evening dress when all the other men were wearing suits, I should be embarrassed. I should feel less at ease than if I had followed the rule. A failing? Of course, but still a human failing. "Cocktail or evening dress?" You ask when you are invited out to dinner. And you are right: there must be a law.

There must be a law, not to stifle originality, but to make it possible. True originality works within the framework of a rule. Racine and Valéry respected the rules of French poetry and were still Racine and Valéry. "A genius has this distinction," said Balzac, "he is just like everyone else and yet no one is like him." And Alain: "Originality in all its forms is merely a way of being like everyone else which defies imitation." I think this is as good a description of male or female elegance as any other.

Yes, the other evening you were like everyone else in that your dress, with its broad green and white panels, was molded in the fashionable line, but there was a dash of boldness in your elegance which belonged to you and you alone. In this way you solved the double problem posed by the delicate question of dress. A young and lovely woman instinctively wants to draw attention because she wants to be attractive even if only to one man. But at the same time the rules of polite society demand, and rightly so, that she resemble other women. (Think of the instant alarm into which the entry of a man in a Grecian tunic would throw a crowded room; picture to yourself the wife of an ambassador arriving at the Théâtre Français in a *paréo*). I think you know how to respect the rules of fashion and how at the same time to make them respect you.

24

Just as within the structure of classical verse the poet preserves the freedom to use the individual coloring of his own words and his own style, so a woman of taste plays endless variations upon the set theme of fashion. A single ornament, a fresh color, a handkerchief gracefully slipped through her belt or knotted round her neck with a studied negligence, a solitary jewel or the deliberate suppression of all jewelry is quite enough for her to write symbolically in her dress, sonnets and rondels as fine as any poet's.

Variety in identity is one of the secrets of all arts. Oh yes, my fair unknown, you may well find the phrase pedantic, but think for a moment. What do musicians compose but variations on a theme? What is Ravel's *Boléro* or any waltz by Chopin? And poets too? They surely have *their* fashion? Lamartine wrote *Le Lac*, Hugo, *La Tristesse d'Olympio*, Musset the *Souvenir*, each one on a favorite theme of his day. You compose your living poem on whatever subject the whim of the hour dictates. You are like all women, but no woman is like you: and that is as it should be. *Adieu*.

A Girl

"Make the conquest of a man," she said. . . . "But women don't make conquests. They are essentially passive. They wait for worship . . . or abuse. Theirs is not the initiative."

"You speak only of the appearance," I said, "not the

25

reality. Long ago Bernard Shaw wrote that if woman awaits but homage, it is as the spider awaits the fly."

"The spider spins her web," she said, "but what can the wretched girl do? Either she is attractive or she isn't. If she is not attractive, none of her poor efforts will ever change a man's feeling for her. In fact, I should think that they would have quite the opposite effect: nothing annoys a boy more than having a girl he doesn't like always around. A woman who offers herself to a man and makes the first advances guarantees his scorn, not his love."

"You would be right," I said, "if the woman were so clumsy as to reveal that the initiative came from her, but the whole art lies in making the first advances without appearing to do so. 'She flies to the willows, making sure her flight is observed.' It is a good old trick of strategy to retreat and draw on your enemy, and girls as well as generals have found it useful."

"In fact, the classic feint," she said. "But if the enemy has not the slightest desire to follow me, my retreat is in vain and there I am left all on my own under the willows."

"There again," I said, "it's up to you as a woman to rouse the man's desire to follow you. There are a hundred and one ways of doing that, which you know far better than I. Grant him a little, pretend to be attracted by him, then suddenly 'drop' him, roughly forbid him what, the evening before, he thought was conquered territory. April weather is fickle, but love and desire thrive on it."

"You discuss this quite coolly," said she, "but your tactics presuppose, first, that the woman who carries them out is quite cold-blooded (and how can you give the man whose very voice makes your heart jump the

26

'fickle April' treatment?) and, second, that the aforesaid male has already begun to pay some attention to you. The kitten won't play unless you throw out your ball of wool."

"I'll never believe," I said, "that a pretty girl is unable to make a man pay her attention, be it only by talking to him about himself. Most males are conceited specialists. Just to listen to them talking about their specialty or themselves is quite enough to make them think you intelligent and want to see you again."

"Must one then," she said, "know how to be bored?"

"Naturally," I said. "It is axiomatic. Whether it is with men, women, love or politics, success in this world goes to those who know how to be bored."

"Then," she said, "I'd prefer to fail."

"Me, too," I said, "but the hell of it is that we'll both succeed."

Such, *querida*, was my conversation with a girl yesterday. What would you? You were not there and life must go on. *Adieu*.

The Male of the Species

The other day I was reading an article in an American newspaper which would have amused you. It was written by a woman for her women readers and she said: "You complain that you can't find a husband? You haven't that all conquering style of beauty to which

27

Hollywood has, alas, accustomed the opposite sex? You live on your own and you don't get much chance to go out and meet people? In short, you know hardly any men, and the eligible ones among them ignore you?

"Let me give you a few tips which I have found very successful. I imagine you live in a little house with a lawn round it in the middle of a group of identical houses. Some of your neighbors are bound to be bachelors.

" 'Of course,' you'll tell me, 'but they ignore my very existence.'

"Wait! This is where my tip becomes useful. Put a ladder up against the wall of your house, climb onto the roof and try to set up a television aerial. That's all you need to do. Before you can turn round all the men in the neighborhood will hurry over like flies to the honey pot. Why? Because men love anything mechanical, because they love fiddling about, because they think they're first-rate handy men . . . and, above all, because they love to demonstrate their superiority over a mere woman.

" 'No,' they'll tell you. 'You don't know how to do it. Let me show you. . . .'

"And naturally you let them. You watch them working for you, with admiration in your eyes. You've made new friends and what's more, you've made them grateful to you for giving them the chance to show off.

"For cutting the grass," my American authoress went on, "I have a power mower which I conscientiously push up and down my lawn. As long as I break my back at the job not a man shows his face. But if I want my neighbors to take an interest in me, it's simplicity itself: I stage a breakdown and pretend to be anxiously looking for the cause of the failure. Next moment one man appears on my right with a pair of pliers and another on my left with a toolbox. Our amateur mechanics are trapped.

"The same game works on the road. Stop, lift the hood and dive bewilderedly among the works. Other flies, greedy for your praise, will stop in their turn to give you the benefit of their experience. But remember that changing a tire or mending a flat will hardly ever attract them. That would be an elementary task, all hard work and no glory. The happiest moment for man, master of the world, is when he can demonstrate his omnipotence to humble woman. How many potential husbands there are driving on their own, only asking, although they may not know it, to find a companion like you, innocent, ignorant, and appreciative. Machines are the signposts on the road to a man's heart."

Actually I think these tips are worth while only when applied to Americans. Would they be as successful in the case of Frenchmen? Perhaps not, but we have *our* weak points. We like to shine in words and in conversation. To ask a financier, a politician, or a man of letters for an explanation of something within his particular province is a form of seduction equally directed at the essential vanity of the male of the species. Skiing or swimming lessons are perfect bait for the outdoor type.

Goethe once remarked that nothing is more charming than study, when the girl is eager to learn and the boy to teach. It is still true. How many love affairs have begun over Latin prose or a chemistry problem, when a girl student's hair brushes the young man's cheek! How potent the spell you weave when you have a knotty point of philosophy explained to you while you listen

29

dreamily showing your profile at the best angle and then prove you have understood! In France the road to the heart is via the mind. Shall I find the road to yours? *Adieu.*

Love and Marriage in France

If you really want to understand the attitude of French men and women toward love and marriage you must first remember the historic attitudes of the French toward these emotions. Your researches will reveal two different currents.

The first, and a very strong one too, is that of sentimental love. In the Middle Ages it was France that first gave birth to *l'amour courtois*. Respect for woman and the desire to win her favor either by songs or poems (troubadours) or by noble deeds have been constant features of a French aristocracy. In no literature have love and passion played such an important role.

But a second and more democratic stream in France has also flowed alongside the first. Rabelais wrote in this tradition. In it physical, sensual love plays a leading part. Marriage is less a question of the emotions than a practical arrangement for raising a family and furthering one's common interests. In Molière the husband is a slightly ridiculous figure whom the wife deceives if she can and who on his side seeks love outside the bonds of marriage.

In the nineteenth century the predominance of a comfortable middle class which attached great importance

30

to money, made marriage a business matter, as Balzac's novels show. Love could follow from living together, from duties shared and from physical accord, but it was not necessary. There were happy marriages which were hardly more than partnerships. The parents and the lawyers discussed the dowry and the marriage contract before the young people had even seen one another.

Today, we have changed all that. Money no longer matters a great deal because a wife who is intelligent and who works, or a husband who is in a good position, are worth infinitely more than a dowry, in a currency that is always insecure. The sentimental stream and the need for romantic love, our centuries old inheritance, have also lost their force. Why? In the first place because emancipated woman is no longer a far-off unknown goddess in man's eyes, she has become his fellow, and in the second place because girls now know the facts of physical love. In so doing they have acquired truer and more healthy ideas about love and marriage.

Young men and women still look for love, but they look for it in marriage. They are suspicious of a marriage of passion for they know that passion hardly ever lasts. In Molière's day marriage was the end of love, today it is the beginning. For the fortunate it is a union more intimate than any former, being at one and the same time physical, intellectual and spiritual. In Balzac's day the husband who loved his lawful wedded wife was a figure of fun; today, novels are more depraved, but life is less so. In a hard world where men and women need every atom of strength for the battle of life, a marriage compounded of companionship, affection and sexual accord appeals more and more to Frenchwomen as the best solution to the problem of love. *Adieu.*

A Sense of Proportion in Adversity

A lady of whom I am very fond tore her velvet dress the other day. It was a subject for high tragedy the whole evening. In the first place she couldn't think how such a broad horizontal tear could have happened. She agreed that the skirt *was* tight, and that when she walked. . . . But all the same Fate had been cruel! It was her nicest dress, the last she had dared order from a famous *couturier*. It was an irreparable blow.

"Why don't you darn it?"

"How like a man! You don't understand, a darn would show terribly."

"Well, then, buy a little black velvet and replace the panel."

"What an idea! Two velvets *never* have the same color or reflection. A black that has been worn takes on a slightly greenish tinge. It would be ghastly. All my friends would say at once that it had been mended."

"When Michelangelo was given a block of marble to carve, he took advantage of the irregularities and made what were faults in the material positive beauties in the execution. Let your tear inspire you. Show your genius: put in a piece of entirely different material. Everyone will think you have done it on purpose and will admire it."

"How naive you are! The eye could bear a discordant note if it were repeated elsewhere on the lapel, the neck or at the waist for example. A panel on its own would look simply absurd. How could I wear an old patched dress?"

In short I had to admit that the disaster was total. Here the moralist stepped into the comforter's shoes.

"Very well," I said. "It's a misfortune, but you must admit that there are worse. Your dress is in tatters? I assure you that I feel for you, but you could have had your stomach perforated or your face cut to shreds in a motor accident: you could have caught pneumonia; you could have been poisoned and, after all, your body is more important than your clothes. You could have lost not a velvet dress, but all your friends. Remember we live in a dangerous age and war could have broken out, then you would run the risk of arrest, imprisonment, deportation, death, disembowelment, atomization. Remember in 1940 you lost, not a yard or two of material, but everything you possessed and then you took your misfortune with a courage which I still admire."

"Where does all this lead?" she said.

"Quite simply to this: the human lot is a hard one, velvet tears, people die, it is all very sad, but one must keep some sense of proportion in adversity. Montaigne wrote: I am perfectly prepared to take their affairs in hand, but not in lungs or liver. By which he meant, 'I, as Mayor of Bordeaux, am quite willing to disentangle your financial matters, but I am not going to do so at the cost of my health.' The same thing applies to your misadventure. I would be only too happy to buy you a new dress, but I refuse to think the loss of the other a national and universal calamity."

Do not, Unknown Lady, destroy your scale of values; do not put a burned soufflé or a run in your stocking on

33

the same footing as the persecution of the innocent or the threat to civilization. *Adieu.*

The Impressionable Age

Grownups live too often on the borders of the world of childhood without trying to explore it. Nevertheless the child for his part closely observes his parents' world, trying to judge and understand it. Words unthinkingly spoken in his presence are stored, interpreted and used to build up a picture of the universe which will last as long as adolescence. A woman remarked in front of her eight-year-old son: "I'm more of a sweetheart than a mother." She had, perhaps, involuntarily wounded him for the rest of his life.

An exaggeration? I don't think so. You may be able to soften the pessimistic view of the universe which a child has formed on what he has experienced in infancy, but your task will be slow and hard. But if, on the contrary, parents have been able to instill into their sons and daughters, from the moment that their minds begin to work, some confidence in the tolerance and good faith of human beings, then they will have helped them to gain a natural aptitude for happiness. Events to come may disappoint those who have led a happy childhood, but in any case they will sooner or later discover for themselves life's tragedies and man's inhuman cruelties. But, contrary to what one might think, they will be

34

better able to face adversity if they have known love and hope.

We say things in front of children which seem harmless enough to us but which appear to them to be full of hidden meaning. An old school mistress once told me that when she asked a little girl, "Pull back the curtain and give us a little light," she saw her pupil hesitate.

"I daren't."

"You daren't? Why not?"

"But . . . I read in the Bible that Rachel died giving light to Benjamin."

A little boy who was always hearing people talk about a Marie Antoinette clock and a Louis XVI salon got it into his head that this particular clock was called Marie Antoinette just as he was called François. One can imagine what weird ideas must have passed through his mind when his first French history lessons told him the grim and tragic story of names which to him were those of everyday objects in his own home.

How many unspoken fears, how many magic incantations float around a child's brain. I remember when I was five or six years old, a touring company announced in the little town where I lived then, the performance of: *Les Surprises du Divorce*. I didn't know what divorce was but I realized at the back of my mind that it was one of those forbidden words, dangerous yet attractive, that unlocked the secrets of the grown-up world. At all events it so happened, that on the day of this performance, a hairdresser in the town, in a fit of jealousy, shot his wife with a revolver. This was discussed in front of me, and I don't know how my childish mind came to associate the two so widely different ideas, but for a long time I firmly believed that divorce was the murder by a

35

husband of the guilty wife, and that this murder was publicly committed on the stage of the theater in Pont-de-l'Eure.

The most careful of parents cannot prevent the growth of strange legends and odd associations of ideas in their child's brain. Experience cannot be transmitted, and each of us must undergo our own apprenticeship in the school of life. But at least we ought not to sow in children's minds seeds which will grow too luxuriantly in that fertile soil. We will spare our children a lot of suffering if we remember that they are far more alert and sensitive than we are. A lesson for mother. *Adieu.*

The Rules of the Game

I do not know whether you occasionally listen on the radio to the *Conversation du samedi*. It is a discussion between Armand Salacrou, Roland Manuel, André Chamson, Claude Mauriac and myself which ranges over a host of subjects: the theater, books we have read, pictures, music and ourselves. In short it is real conversation, completely spontaneous; we talk exactly as though we were five friends meeting round a café table. For my part I enjoy it immensely and am always delighted to meet my companions each week at the microphone. Alain said that friendship is born from constraint: the school, or the army; this enforced appointment has made us friends.

36

The other day Claude Mauriac, in the course of our discussion, defended an argument which I think just. *"L'amour courtois"* he said, to quote him more or less accurately, "the ideal of the romances of chivalry was a game whose rules have hardly changed since the Courts of Love. You find them again in the seventeenth century: in *L'Astrée* and *La Princess de Clèves;* they are the same, though given more emphasis, among the romantics; they still determine the words and deeds of Marcel Proust's Swann. This tradition demands that lovers should be jealous of both body and mind; that every word of the beloved should be analyzed, her every gesture interpreted; that the slightest frown on the face of the loved one should upset them; that they should grow pale at the thought of desertion. Molière made fun of these agonies, Proust suffered from them: but writers and their public were for hundreds of years in perfect agreement on the nature of these rules. This, then, is what seems to me to be new in the outlook of young authors of today, namely that they no longer accept the rules of the game. Not that they no longer play the game of love, but that they have altered the code that governs it. The body on which the whole world can freely gaze no longer inspires jealousy."

Here I broke in to quote a letter from Victor Hugo to his fiancée, a letter which could never in fact have been written today, in which he bitterly reproaches her for having lifted her dress to prevent its being soiled in the street and in so doing exposed her ankle. He, Hugo, was so angry at this that he could have killed a passer-by who glanced at the white silk stocking, or even killed himself. For our young novelists the rule of the game seems to be to eliminate all jealousy and cynically to dis-

37

cuss the affairs of the woman they love, something quite incompatible with *l'amour courtois*, which is an emotion that excludes all else, "person to person" as the telephone operators say, and is a game for two and two only.

But, in point of fact, in the second half of the modern novel the lovers generally discover what love is. They recognize, half regretfully, the charms of fidelity, the pleasure of true feeling, and even the agony of jealousy. But being more self-conscious than Romantic lovers, or even those of Proust, they discuss these things with an air of detachment and a certain irony, at least verbally. They spice love with comedy, a discordant mixture, but one that has its peculiar charm.

Is this new? I am not certain. From Madame de La Fayette to Louise de Vilmorin the rules of the game have never been absolute. The Anglo-Saxons have for a long while refused to express their deepest feelings. One can observe, side by side with courtly tradition, that of the Renaissance. The loves of Benvenuto Cellini and even of Ronsard, were not Romantic. Certain of Stendhal's heroes, and, in our day some of Montherlant's, play the game according to Renaissance rules not those of the Courts of Love. But the rules of the game have often changed and they will go on changing. I await the young man who writes a modern *Adolphe* or a modern *Swann;* I predict vast success for him. For if the rules alter, the prize remains the same. The prize is you, dearest. *Adieu.*

Making the Most of One's Disadvantages

Have you noticed, my soul's unknown, that one can please as much by one's faults as by one's virtues? And sometimes please more easily? It is because your good qualities, in elevating you, depress "him," while your defects, in giving him the chance to laugh at you, raise him in his own eyes. A woman can be forgiven for prattling, but not for being in the right. Byron left his wife, whom he nicknamed the Princess of Parallelograms, because she was too wise and clear-sighted. The Greeks bore a grudge against Aristides because he was called the Just.

In his *Choses vues*, Victor Hugo mentions a certain Monsieur de Salvandy, whose career, from the worldly point of view, was one of unbroken success. He became in turn a minister, a member of the Academy, an ambassador and a Grand Cross of the Legion of Honor. You may say that that is not very much, but he was successful too with women, and that is much more important. Yet when he entered the great world under the wing of Madame Gail, the famous Sophie Gay exclaimed: "But my dear, your young man is a mass of absurdities. You'll have to take him in hand." "Good heavens," cried Madame Gail, "don't remove those. What will he have left? They are the very means by which he will rise." And events proved Madame Gail was right.

39

Henry de Jouvenel once told me that in his younger days, when he was a journalist, he was struck by the Parliamentary debut of a deputy from the Calvados, Henri Chéron. Chéron, potbellied, bearded and frock-coated, would leap onto the table and break into the *Marseillaise* and he favored a pompous style of oratory. Clemenceau made him Undersecretary of State for War, whereupon Chéron paid a round of visits to barracks where he would sample the soldiers' stew. He was the talk of all the messes and Jouvenel, thinking that it would be amusing to write an article on him, went to see him. Chéron received him defiantly.

"Young man," he said. *"I know perfectly well that you will describe me as a fool. Very well, do so. Yes, I am ridiculous, but* of my own free will, *for remember this, young man, absurdity in this country is the one form of notoriety* which is not fatal."

It was a remark which would have enchanted Sten-dhal. Without going to the extent of absurdity, have you not noticed that little fads and oddities of dress do more to establish a man or a woman in the eyes of the world than genius? Thousands who never read a word of his books, knew all about Gide's sombrero and Mexican cape. Winston Churchill is a great orator, but he knows human nature and cunningly plays upon it with his unusual hat, and his Victory V sign. I knew a French ambassador to London who spoke no English, but he wore a loosely spotted bow tie which enchanted the English; he made the grade.

Watch people dining in a restaurant. Who is the man who gets the best service, around whose table the head-waiter hovers? Is it the reasonable man who is always satisfied? Not a bit of it; it is the customer with the fads

To be demanding is to show interest. *Moral*: Be natural, and, if it is your bent, be picturesque. People will thank you for it. *Adieu*.

Scenes

Do you have scenes with your husband or your friends? Despite your Minervan air, I should be surprised if you did not. By making a scene, a woman achieves, in one moment of abandon, what she might have gone on asking for in a reasonable way for years. But she must know the kind of man with whom she is dealing.

There are hot-blooded men who are feminine on this point and who love a scene. They answer violence with violence and the harshest things are said. But when it is all over the tension will have been relaxed, the feelings relieved and there will be a certain charm about making up the quarrel. I know quite a number of women who in such circumstances are not even afraid of physical violence. They would never admit as much, but they instinctively invite it. The remark, "Well, and if I like being beaten?" is profoundly true. For women who like their men to be powerful, in character as well as in physique, whatever rough handling they receive will merely serve to stimulate their love.

"How horrible!" you say. "I would never see again any man who struck me."

41

You really believe it, but to be quite sure you must put it to the proof. If it confirms your repugnance, it shows that your body is more a source of pride than a physical pleasure to you.

The normal man has a horror of scenes. They put him in a position of inferiority because he is generally on the defensive. How can a husband, in cold blood, successfully answer a flood of invective spewed forth by an angry priestess? When the tempest bursts about their heads, the majority take refuge either in flight or in deaf ears behind a newspaper, for a scene without a touch of genius quickly becomes monotonous.

The very word *scene* should guide us. It is a term borrowed from the theater. To make a scene really effective it must be well staged. Founded on a trifle and because the mounting tension must find a release, it should gather, drawing strength from every remembered slight, swell with an accumulation of half-buried grievances, fill the air with tears and then die away at the right moment, return from tears through melancholy to smiles, to draw to a voluptuous close.

"But that means that the whole scene is contrived, that the woman is always mistress of herself . . ."

Of course, "theater" was the word we used. A capable actress is always conscious of what she says and does. The most successful scenes are always deliberately provoked and artificially carried through. This is not only true of women, great leaders of men such as Napoleon or Marshall Lyautey rarely lost their tempers, and then only when they felt it absolutely necessary. But on those occasions their fury bore down all obstacles. In moments like this Lyautey would go so far as to throw his marshal's kepi to the ground and trample it underfoot. On such days he would tell his batman: "Give me my old kepi."

Follow his example. Reserve your anger for important occasions: husband your tears. Scenes only produce their full effect if they are rare. In countries where storms are an everyday occurrence nobody pays any attention to them. I would not set myself up as an example, but it is a fact that I am naturally even-tempered. Now I find that once or twice a year some egregious injustice or stupidity shatters my calm, and on those days all yield to me. Surprise is one of the secrets of victory. Let your scenes be few, but brilliant. *Adieu.*

The Golden Nail

At last you have answered my letters. But naturally not under your own name. The Unknown keeps her incognito for me. At least I know your handwriting and I like it. I love those firm, clear, open letters. It is the hand of an honest man.

And of an honest woman? Perhaps! But that needs looking into, for in introducing yourself you ask me an odd question.

"For five years," you write, "I have had a friend. He is tender and witty and he visits me nearly every day, chooses my books and my entertainments, in short he fills my life delightfully. I am not his mistress and I do not want to be, yet that is what he asks, insistently, and

43

it tortures me. He tells me that my pride rules my passions, that he suffers too much for this to go on, and that in the end he will stop seeing me. Must I yield to this blackmail? It is a nasty word, but it describes his actions perfectly, for he knows I need his friendship. Doesn't he prize mine highly enough to accept it as it is offered him?"

I don't know if you have read a short novel, *Le Clou d'or* which Sainte-Beuve wrote for the sole purpose of overcoming the scruples of a woman with whom he found himself in precisely the same position as your friend is with you. Here was an attractive young woman, with something almost virginal about her, childless and younger than her age, who made him suffer torments by refusing to surrender. He begged her to grant him all. "At the age of thirty or forty to possess a woman whom one has long known and loved, be it only once, is what I call sealing friendship with a golden nail," he told her.

Sainte-Beuve claimed that an attachment riveted by this golden nail would last longer, for a lifetime perhaps, than one which relied on gratitude, affection or intellectual harmony. To support his opinion he quoted a good eighteenth century author. "If two people who, while not necessarily being in love have a liking for each other, if these two enjoy but fifteen minutes' intimacy they will have created thereby such mutual confidence, destroying the barriers of reserve between them, as the warmest friendship could not display even after ten years' space."

The problem of the golden nail is your own. I realize that it is your friend who raises it, as did Sainte-Beuve in Sophie Loyré d'Arbouville's day. For a man it is the torment of Tantalus to be in the clutches of a coquette

44

(perhaps, unaware of the role she plays), who perpetually offers him bliss and perpetually leaves him
unsatisfied. Nevertheless, I do not believe in the golden
nail. In such affairs the first attempt is seldom the most
successful. You need a whole bag of nails.

In point of fact, if your friend suffered as much as he
claims, he would have overcome your resistance long
ago. Women understand instinctively which of their
hangers-on they will be able to keep as friends without
ever granting them a single favor. It may surprise them
slightly (an Englishwoman gave me this definition of
Platonic love: "We ask ourselves what he wants, and he
wants nothing"), but they are happy enough with the
way things are, and they take advantage of the situation.
But once the real lover comes on the scene, exit these
friendly shadows. Once Chateaubriand had made her fall
in love, Juliette Récamier was his and his alone. She had
long sought to keep the bloom of his affection; in the end
she found that the fruit too is good. Take guidance from
that if you can. The best oracles speak in riddles. *Adieu.*

The Lecturer Arrives

       "Do you think that's the one?"
"I'm positive it is."
"He doesn't *look* like an author."
"He's anxious, he's looking for us. . . . Good evening!"
"Oh! Good evening. . . . You're Monsieur Bernard?"

45

"Yes, *cher maître*, and this is my wife. . . . She would-
n't believe it was you. . . . You look so much older than
your photograph. Not too tired after your trip?"

"Exhausted. A whole day on the train. A scrappy
lunch. Anyway I've two clear hours before the lecture:
at least I shall be able to have a rest."

"Not quite two hours. Before I take you to the hotel I
must show you the lecture room. You'll want to see it."

"Good heavens, no. Since I can't change it. . . ."

"I'm awfully sorry, *cher maître*, but we must go. I've
arranged for you to meet Monsieur Blavski, the cinema
owner . . . Monsieur Blavski is very touchy. In any case
it would be much better if I explained one or two things
when we're actually there. It's a large room, but the
acoustics aren't good. . . . You have to speak very loudly
and stand beside the table looking slightly to the left."

"I hope at least the place is warm. I've just had flu
and my doctor . . ."

"I'm afraid not, there *is* a furnace, but it doesn't work.
However, when the hall is full, it warms up quickly.
Unfortunately there won't be many people there
tonight."

"The advance sale has been bad?"

"Very bad. . . . Barely twenty-five or thirty seats.
Don't worry, *cher maître*, when I saw how disastrous
it was, I gave away free tickets to the schools and the
army camp so that it wouldn't look so bare."

"Is it always like this?"

"Oh, no! We've had some marvelous successes. But
this evening Jacques Thibaud is giving a concert in the
Town Hall, and then a touring company is performing
Les Temps difficiles at the theater. Well, a lecture, naturally."

46

"But couldn't you have come to some arrangement with the concert promoters and the theater manager?"

"Ah, politics. You know what these local quarrels are. . . . In any case we wouldn't have had much of an audience. It's hardly the subject to attract people. *Stendhal's Novels* . . . I don't want to seem discouraging but you must admit. . . . No, the sort of lecture that goes down well here is: *Popular Songs in 1900*, with phonograph records, or *Love in Turkey*. At all events, I'm quite sure what you will have to say will be very interesting and people won't regret having come. The only thing is, it's rather a nuisance for our society, we're not very well off."

"I'm terribly sorry. But candidly when I saw from your letterhead that you called yourselves: The Society of Literature and the Arts, I thought that Stendhal . . ."

"I will explain, *cher maître*. The Literary Society is just a group of friends that I organized. We like to make the acquaintance, at a lecture, of a famous man . . . or even a fairly well-known one. For example, even if this evening's lecture is a failure, we shall be very glad to have had you to dinner."

"What? Is there a dinner party?"

"Yes, at half past seven."

"But I never have anything to eat before a lecture."

"Do just as you please. We'll eat and you can talk."

"Dinner at half-past seven? It's nearly seven as it is! At all events will it be possible for me to wear the clothes I've traveled in?"

"The committee will be in lounge suits, but the lecturer wears a dinner jacket: we make it a rule. In any case you've all the time in the world. The lecturer is billed for eight-thirty but people here are never on time.

Even if you started at nine-fifteen most of the audience wouldn't come in until after you had begun."

"Then I'll be free about ten-fifteen?"

"Well, after the lecture some of our friends will certainly want you to autograph their copies of your books. Then at eleven o'clock Monsieur Perche would like you to take a glass of champagne with him."

"Who is Monsieur Perche?"

"What? You don't know Monsieur Perche? But he told us he was at school with you!"

"If he says so, it is doubtless true. But, please, ask Monsieur Perche for old acquaintance's sake to forego his generous plan. I must get some rest."

"Impossible, *cher maître*. Monsieur Perche is one of our patrons. This is the room. No, the poster is for the film."

Querida, if you must know I have been on a lecture tour this week and I have come home worn out. *Adieu*.

Bachelors

I once knew an old politician who would always say that the man of action should never marry. "Look at the facts," he would tell me. "Why, despite all the difficulties in my career, have I preserved my calm and serenity? Simply because every evening after the battles of the day I could sit down, open a book and for-

48

get; because I had no jealous and ambitious wife beside me to remind me of my colleagues' successes, and to retail all the malicious gossip of the salons which other wives told her about me. The single man is happy."

He never convinced me. Obviously the single man has far fewer responsibilities. He is spared a home and family and he is not liable, on the day he needs it most, to find his energy sapped by the illness of one of his children or by a domestic quarrel. But is a bachelor really free from all the whims of womankind? Unless he is a saint there is always someone in his life and he may well find a mistress far more dangerous than any lawful wedded wife.

A wife, at least, has the same stake in life as her husband. They have grown old together and she has come to understand him. The mistress, chosen for her youth and beauty, is far more likely to give her elderly lover cause for anxiety. Naturally there are exceptions to this rule. The great American actress, Ruth Draper, in one of her inimitable sketches, shows the businessman in the triangle of hateful wife, efficient secretary and gentle, restful mistress. All things are possible and wives can be quarrelling machines. In practice though, it is rare enough. Turn to English history; nearly all her great statesmen have been married. Lady Peel, Lady Beaconsfield and Mrs. Gladstone were all admirable wives. In France Guizot, Thiers, Poincaré, in short, the most "solid" of our statesmen, were married. It is true that Gambetta and Briand were not, but who knows whether, had they been married, they might not have played a still more important part in history?

The bachelor will always be incomplete in that he will see one half of human kind only through critical or

49

TO AN UNKNOWN LADY

romantic eyes. Furthermore he does not have the chance
to see the way children grow up, their education and
their needs. Is he a whole man? In that fine novel of his,
Les Célibataires, Montherlant rubs in the harsh truth that
the bachelor is nearly always ignorant of the real world
in which he lives and that his narrow universe is like a
ball on a piece of elastic perpetually rebounding onto itself. One can answer that by saying that Balzac was a
bachelor for most of his life, in spite of which no one
could portray married life better than he. True, but
Balzac was Balzac and ten sentences were enough for
him to bring a family to life. The average man is hard
put to it in fifty years of marriage to understand just one
woman. *Adieu.*

Novels

You ask me how to write a novel? If I
knew I wouldn't write them. This is not a play on words.
What I want to say is this: any novelist who takes too
great a heed of his technique will be in a state of mortal
sin.

There are made-up novels. Such and such an author
has some thesis to maintain. One character represents
Evil (the traitor in melodrama, or the "salaud" in the
Existentialist novel): another embodies Virtue, Liberty,
the Faith or the Revolution (for times change and with

them the hero's nature). In the end Good, whatever it may be, is the winner and the novelist the loser.

Someone else has a tested formula. *Take a girl, as beautiful and as touching as possible. After great misfortune give her the chance of meeting her knight. Give her a femme-fatale for rival. Long drawn-out struggles. Sudden changes of fortune. Season with sex, varied to suit the public taste. Go on writing this novel all your life. By the time you have churned out twenty, your fortune will be made.*

A third will choose some period in history, for preference one which combines a strong dramatic and sex interest. (The prisons of the French Revolution provide an adequate background, with passion under the shadow of the guillotine: The Wars of the First Empire with its victories in love and war: Restoration England with its debauchery: the reign of Louis XV or the Regency with its Parc-aux-Cerfs and its private dinners: the Second Empire with its great courtesans). Once you have picked your period, you have only to place in it a heroine who is as lovely as she is heartless and cynical, and then put her to bed with a different man every thirty pages. Guaranteed sale—a hundred thousand copies. Change the century every three books.

These recipes will bring you a fortune but not a masterpiece. The wells of beauty lie hidden underground. The true novel springs from an inner compulsion. Stendhal and Balzac enjoyed writing stories which enabled them to recreate their own lives under different disguises. Fabrice in *La Chartreuse de Parme* is Stendhal as the young and handsome Italian nobleman; *Lucien Leuwen*, Stendhal the good looking lieutenant, the millionaire banker's son. "A writer compensates as best he can for

51

the injustice of his lot." At times it is hard to strip away the mask. "I am *Madame Bovary*" said Flaubert. And that is why *Madame Bovary* is a masterpiece.

How does a novelist recognize that a subject is, for him, worth while? In this way: it stimulates him whenever he thinks about it. If the theme touches a nerve, a memory of sorrow, or sometimes of great happiness, his book will have a chance of being good. But on two conditions: first he must stand back a little from his subject, or, as Balzac says, allow time for gestation. "Poetry is emotion recollected in tranquillity." The time for writing a novel is not the moment your lover deserts you. The wound still bleeds, you must close it, not reopen it. When it has healed, you find a pleasurable pain in tickling it. It will not be sufficiently painful to make you cry, but will still hurt enough to make you sing, in the poetic sense I mean, which is the sense of the novelist.

The second condition is that you should not approach your subject directly. My Unknown, if you want to write a novel do not make it your own life story unaltered. Modesty would, I hope, prevent you. Tell a story near enough to your own to enable you to express your feelings while at the same time preserving the illusion that a mask protects you. And if you succeed, don't send me your manuscript: I should only lose it. *Adieu.*

The Unforgiving Minute

My fair Unknown, it is not true to say that our lives are determined from our birth or even from all eternity by a mysterious and all-powered force. To a certain extent they are, I agree. Had you been born ugly, your lot would have been very different, and your beauty itself is the result of the mingling of hereditary chromosomes on which your free will can have had no influence. Then, too, one must add that today a face can be shaped by plastic surgery, that grace and wit can beautify and that mental serenity is reflected in the looks. Who was it then who said that after forty every man is responsible for his own face? Yet above all it is in the way in which we react to events that our power to reshape our destiny resides.

Events are no more than events. A man may love you, and tell you that he does. A war may take him away from you, a slump may ruin him, another woman take his fancy. These are facts, but by themselves they make you neither happy nor unhappy. What will your attitude be towards them? That is the crucial point. In many situations, there is one moment and one moment only, in which the decision you make of your own free will alters the whole course of your life. That is what I call *the unforgiving minute*. Why one minute only? Life is like that. We are seldom given a second chance.

53

This is true in war. The Marne was one such brief opportunity. Von Kluck had advanced too rapidly. Joffre and Gallieni were able to take advantage of this. That day, though none yet knew it, Germany had lost the war. But it is nonetheless true in the war between the sexes. There is often a fleeting moment in which a man who has long courted a woman sees in her eyes the tenderness and surrender that somehow shows him his cause is won. A thousand factors have contributed to this: the lucky chance of a tête-à-tête, a tone of voice, a recently read book, a storm in the air, a gesture. In short her defences are down.

But if, at this of all moments, we let the chance go by with the thought: The time will come again, perhaps even more favorably, then we shall have lost our opportunity, and lost it forever. Our friend will recover her self-control, will think of the dangers, and will despise our lack of enterprise. Above all she will no longer be under the influence of the extraordinarily favorable set of circumstances that inclined her towards surrender. This evening victory was easy and certain; tomorrow it will be impossible.

What made me think about this unforgiving minute was my rereading yesterday of Meredith's fine novel: *The Tragic Comedians*. It is the story of the German Socialist Ferdinand Lassalle, who loved the daughter of a noble family and who by his good looks as much as by his genius was able to make her love him. "My family hates you. We must elope!" she told him one day. He objected: "Why let a scandal wreck your life? Be patient for a few more months and we shall marry, with your parents' consent." He never gained either that consent or the girl for his wife. What is more, he was killed

54

in a duel by her fiancé. What a strange part pride and passion play! Lassalle, jilted, died like a fool in an affair of honor. The girl mourned him too late. Then she married the man who had killed him.

Too late. Never give these two dreadful words the chance to haunt you. I know a lady, who, during the last war, received a proposal from an officer she loved. She asked for one night to consider her answer, and the next day wrote her acceptance. But the next day was May 10, 1940, the day of the German offensive. The officer had been recalled to the front; her letter went astray: In despair through the double destruction of his country and his love, he courted Death, that kind-hearted creature whom no one ever courts in vain. For the woman all that was left was remorse and regret, because he was the man she had always wanted to marry, and only pride and respect for convention had made her ask for the delay. Would she not have done better to have said *yes* then and there?

Moral: write to me at once. *Adieu.*

Nonsense Stories

Do you like André Gide? For my own part I used to find him a companion whose culture and boundless curiosity fascinated me. Later on I lost touch with the man, who had disappointed me, although I never passed so harsh a judgment on him as have certain

55

books published since his death. In them Gide is seen as the cold egoist, so much the man of letters as to be scarcely human, obsessed by his unnatural loves and sometimes so eccentric as to verge on madness. "I thought you were a sick man or a lunatic," his wife told him during their virginal honeymoon. And yet. . . .

And yet his charm was real. In his last books, *Ainsi soit-il* or *Les Jeux sont faits*, written in fits and starts and as though dictated by a planchette board, side by side with the "inveterate pridefulness" as he called it, the disconcerting egocentricity, there are a thousand delightful little touches. I love the sound of his laugh, it stayed so young right to the end. It is often surprising to discover what amuses a great mind or at any rate one who wished to be considered as such, and whom a multitude of readers the world over accorded that title. Would you like to hear a few of the stories he enjoyed?

A cock is striding impatiently up and down the waiting room of a maternity hospital, cigarette in beak, wing tips clasped behind his back like Napoleon. The floor is littered with cigarette ends. The door opens and a hen in nurse's uniform pops her head in. She leans forward and whispers confidentially: "It's an egg."

Another: A man and his dog are playing chess in a café. The dog is setting out the pieces with the end of his paw, when up comes an astonished spectator!

"But your dog really plays! He is intelligent . . ."

The man interrupts: "Why exaggerate? He lost the last two games!"

A third of Gide's stories: the scene is a movie house. A gentleman discovers that the lady sitting next to him is accompanied by a bear, a real tame bear. In the interval the animal goes out for a few minutes and the man leans forward.

"Excuse me, Madame, is that really a bear with you?"

"But, of course!"

"And does he like the film?"

"He hasn't said anything about it yet, all I can tell you is that he enjoyed the book very much."

You recognize the typical nonsense story. Essentially it consists of taking the absurdest proposition as fact and pretending to pass it off by exaggerating it still more. Does this sort of story amuse you as much as it does me? I will add two more which I have taken not from Gide but from the common stock from which he drew his own.

It is lunch time, on the table is a dish of spinach. One of the guests takes it, turns it upside down and puts it on his head. Showered in green water, he notices the astonishment of his neighbors. Then, rather embarrassed:

"I beg your pardon," he tells them. "I thought it was the mashed potatoes."

One final story. New York: a room in which a Negro lies fast asleep. The telephone rings.

"Is that Regent 7-0235?"

"No!"

The Negro goes back to bed again. Once more the telephone rings.

"Is that Regent 7-0235?"

"No! No!"

The other in confusion: "Oh, I beg your pardon—I'm so sorry to have woken you up."

But the Negro answers good-humoredly: "That

57

doesn't matter. I had to get up anyway to answer the telephone."

But perhaps you are impervious to their comic absurdity. In that case you have my condolences. *Adieu.*

Clothe the Naked

George Moore, the great English writer, told me one day that having found this phrase "I saw a lady on the beach entirely unclothed" in one of Henry James' books he asked the American novelist: "Why unclothed, James? Naked is surely the proper word. Nakedness is man's natural state: clothes only come later." James, a pompous, serious-minded man, thought a moment and then replied: "You are wrong, Moore. In a civilized country, man's natural state is to be clothed. Nakedness is abnormal."

I have just met the same idea in a doubtless forgotten essay by Alain-Fournier on the female form. "A woman's body," he writes, "is not the pagan idol, the naked courtesan that Pierre Louys has dug up in ancient Greece." To the little boy in the Christian era, the essence of the female form is the dress, the skirt and the blouse. "We shall not get to know the body better by unclothing it; for hundreds of years in our climate it has been covered: from childhood we know it by what it wears." And even in its nakedness a woman's body would not, in Alain-Fournier's view, be deprived of the aura of dress. "The stiff, chaste clothes which we see in medieval stained-glass would have left their imprint and the limbs would emerge, slightly stiff, gently elongated, almost unfleshed."

This was written at the beginning of the century: since then our beaches have become littered with naked flesh, the cinema has thrown open beauty competitions to thousands of spectators, and the sculptured nudity of the Greek nymph has ceased to be an attraction for men of today. Such license is however purely relative. One country may tolerate an exposure of the breasts, while another would never allow it. André Billy has published a little book, *Pudent*, in which he has collected a variety of passages that illustrate the variations in feeling. Is modesty natural? Certainly not in the animal world. Many species hide themselves when they mate, as birds of prey do when they drink, but this is because they are vulnerable at such moments. They are not ashamed of their bodies.

Why is man more bashful? Partly because for him there is no mating season and it would be dangerous for society to allow his desires to be aroused on any and every occasion. What horrible promiscuity would there be in families if modesty did not exist. The overpowering emotions which nudity arouses are chastened by clothes. How could one dictate sensible letters to one's secretary if she were stark naked?

"But don't you think," someone will say, "that familiarity lessens the temptations? On the beach who takes a scrap of notice of all the perfectly shaped thighs and breasts?"

59

"The beach is for rest and enjoyment not for work and thought."

André Billy gives another reason for clothing the naked, that is the need women have of defending their own prestige. "Defence is a seasoning that spices the sauce," said Montaigne. And Stendhal: "Modesty flatters the lover. He says to himself: What a fine fellow I am! She casts aside all her inhibitions for me!" Billy concludes: "The woman whom I guess to be the most modest interests me because I guess that her modesty goes with a romantic melancholy.... How extravagantly will a woman who is jealous of the secrets of her body lavish her emotions." I think as he does: far greater pleasure would come from making love with the very timid Madame de Rênal, who had to overcome enormous inhibitions before she could bring herself to surrender, than with the divine Countess de Castiglione who exposed her body to all her friends as though it were a work of art.

There is another hypothesis, namely that modesty is fear of showing one's imperfections. Is it true and have you noticed that women with good figures are less modest than others? A woman whose education and religion have made her chaste will remain so whatever her physical perfections. No, the truth is that nudity is unnatural. It is impossible, said the terrible Dr. Swift, to imagine a Parliament of naked men. I would not wish that spectacle upon you. *Adieu.*

The Shadow Line

You go forward and times goes forward with you until you see before you a shadow line which warns you that now you must leave behind you the things of your youth. Conrad, who wrote the phrase, places the shadow line across man's fortieth year. Émile Henriot, in his brilliant novel *Tout va finir*, shows that it is nearer the fiftieth, and of the two he is, I think, the one who is right. His hero describes "the awful feeling one has of going down hill, that all is in vain, that nothing can stop the skid towards Death."

"You'll say I'm neurotic," he tells his doctor, "No, it isn't that. I've been a confirmed optimist all my life, Doctor. I've a horror of being sorry for myself, of asking for sympathy. But really there is something wrong."

"How old are you?" asks the doctor.

"Forty-eight, nearly forty-nine."

"Yes, this always starts about that age."

I think that most men, even those who in the eyes of their fellows seem to enjoy unbroken success, pass through a crisis of despair the moment they cross the shadow line. However brilliant a man's life may be, there is always an immense difference between the dreams of boyhood and the reality of manhood. Not one of us follows the path he has chosen without ever leaving it. As the molecules of gas are turned from their trajectory at every instant of their flight by innumerable collisions so, at every moment of their lives, human beings are at the mercy of chance.

61

"Whatever happens," says the young man, "there is one thing I shall *not* do." Meet him thirty years later and that is precisely the thing he *has* done. Thirty years ago the pretty girl said: "The one thing I shall never let myself become is a wife who is deceived and who puts up with it." Now she is a dull, graying matron, left alone more and more, and she puts up with it.

"Soon I shall be fifty," wrote Stendhal sadly, and he counted the women he had loved. However much he tried to delude himself, they were still all second-rate. When he was twenty, he had pictured his love life as being a series of encounters on the highest plane. And his tenderness, his knowledge of love and his pride had deserved them. But the heroines he had wished for never came, and unable to live his own novels, Stendhal had had to make do with writing them. Only, when he crossed the shadow line he wept for the mistresses he had never had.

Soon I shall be fifty, thinks the writer. What has he achieved? What has he written? It seems that he has still everything to say and that only now can he see clearly the books that he must write. But how many years of work are still left in him? He suffers from blood pressure already. His eyes refuse to read. Ten, fifteen years? "Art is long: life is short." The phrase which he once thought so commonplace now comes to him pregnant with meaning. Has he still the leisure, like Proust, to set forth on the discovery of time past?

Young men, so prodigal of their time should sometimes remember that like us they must cross the shadow line. And as for you, *querida*. . . .

But women seem not to see the shadow line. *Adieu*.

Incompatibility in Marriage

       Incompatibility is a conflict of character and of temperament which prevents two people agreeing, and even less, living together. Where true incompatibility exists, this conflict cannot be resolved and were that not so, it would be given another name. In some cases, at the start of married life, husband and wife find it difficult, though not impossible, to get used to each other. Sometimes it is because they are not really in love. A man and a woman have made a sensible marriage, yet both of them are used to living alone and running their own lives without reference to anyone else; they find it hard to put up with the sudden restraint imposed by having to consider the other partner's desires and plans. Love would make the sacrifice easy and their life would acquire fresh patterns. If such love is not there from the start, their resistance will prove too strong for it. At all events if love is born from their living together, or if their good sense plays its conciliatory part, all will turn out well. But incompatibility becomes complete when, after a few months, or perhaps even years, it becomes evident that time cannot work the slightest change upon an opposition whose roots go too deep.

This may be caused by a wide variety of things: in the first place, conflict of taste. Living together requires a minimum of common ground. Take the case of George Sand. As a girl of eighteen she married Baron Casimir Dudevant. He was a pleasant enough young man: he wanted to make her happy and she for her part entered upon marriage with the best intentions in the world. But she was a cultivated woman, she adored music and reading. As soon as Casimir opened a book, he started to nod. Since he admired his wife, he made every effort to please her. She suggested he should read Pascal, whereupon he tried to follow her recommendation. Alas! The book slipped from his fingers and his wife despised him.

She, for her part, had read any number of novels and she believed that life should be like them. She asked and expected love to be a thing of passion expressed in terms of the sublime. But poor Casimir was quite ignorant of the vocabulary of ecstasy. To him, in married life, love was a right. The husband took his wife in his arms and that was that. Incompatibility. It was not hard to predict that, in spite of good will on both sides, this marriage would founder on the first rock it struck, and that the rock in question would be a romantic young man.

In certain cases the conflict is neither one of the intellect nor of the feelings: it stems from a difference in background. The husband has been raised by careful, economical parents: the wife by a happy-go-lucky mother. She cannot run a home. Household accounts bore her, and she cannot see the sense in a family budget. Their conflicts will be ceaseless and will soon become unpleasant. The husband will want her to keep a written account of her expenses and balance it against her receipts. The wife will think this just a form of niggardly and petty tyranny. If neither party is prepared to compromise, their quarrel can produce incompatibility. The same thing will happen where the rhythm of life differs strongly in two people. Imagine a keen and active husband, a rapid worker who must have a life fully occupied, with something going on the whole time, travel, entertainment; and harness him to a wife, who is weak-willed, slow thinking, eternally tired and always anxious to rest. He is always on time, to the very minute: she is always late, quite indifferent to the hour of the day. How can one avoid the conflicts that must arise from these differences in the pressure of life? Mutual tolerance might be the answer but only at the cost of mutual suffering. If a common ground is not established, if physical love does not yoke this uneven pair the result will be incompatibility.

Husbands and wives run a big risk too when, although they may share to a large degree the same habits and tastes, they bring under the same roof political ideologies or religious beliefs that are utterly opposed. In certain ages such things are not held important, but such periods are rare and short, and in our own time we must take sides in these questions. It is true that one can imagine the devout wife who tolerates her slightly agnostic husband or the socialist husband who does the same for his more conservative wife. But will such tolerance last? Ideas motivate deeds and these the other partner will blame. Political leanings bring a host of friends who support the same party. The friends of the one become the foes of the other. Once again true love can give the chance of reconciliation. Without it, it is much better not to take the risk. Marry a man (or a woman) who thinks, not exactly, but very nearly as you do about essentials. If you don't, incompatibility lies in wait for you. *Adieu*.

For a married couple the most serious mal-adjustments, as you can imagine, are those which arise from unbalanced sexual relations. For example a sensualist, in whose life physical love is of prime importance marries a girl of whose feelings on the matter he knows nothing. And how should he know? She is a virgin and is herself equally ignorant. It happens that, perhaps because her husband is clumsy in his technique or perhaps because she is herself temperamentally cold, she gets no pleasure from what is her husband's greatest delight. If she has dexterity and good health, she can accept her position of giving a pleasure every night in which she cannot share. Many first-rate marriages are founded on such a compromise. But if it is the man who is the chilly lover, there can be no remedy. In both cases it is to be feared that the partner who is frustrated will seek elsewhere the pleasure his marriage denies him. This is one of the most serious forms of incompatibility.

How can it be prevented? By reflecting on the hidden causes of such discord, reflections which can guide us as much in the choice of a mate as in the art of getting along with him. A great many human beings are more liable than others to these sexual inhibitions. They are those who, for one reason or another, think that they are being humiliated. In secret they nurse a danger-ous pride, and this pride will make up for whatever defects they may have. Someone who is weak-willed becomes very aggressive to disguise his weakness. In particular there are plenty of women who feel a sort of resentment because they belong to the sex which was, for so long, treated in a way they think offensive. Today they should be appeased by the legal equality which they have at last gained. But no. Centuries of slavery have left their mark. And in any case even today is their equality real? Are there not still many women who, in or outside marriage, are compelled to a loveless surrender of their bodies? The special features surrounding women's lot have become less marked, but, according to Simone de Beauvoir, they have not yet disappeared.

Hence some women feel intolerably humiliated, and often without knowing it they bear a grudge against the husband who is also their master. They get no pleasure from sex because unconsciously they reject it. It is absurd, but once again they would feel enslaved if they really surrendered to it. All the same these women can be happy and make their husbands happy. But only on two conditions: they must either marry a weakling whom they can dominate or, on the contrary, they must marry a man strong and intelligent enough to undertake the soothing of their hypersensitive self-esteem. The conquest of such a woman is a fascinating exercise, slowly rebuilding her self-confidence and curing her inferiority complex. Then the barriers of pride gradually collapse and pleasure, which demands a humble surrender, is born. My dearest, my only wish is for you to be a humble servant of love. Servant and Mistress— *Adieu.*

Stories of the Theater

Are you fond of actors? I like them enormously and I find them the best company of all. I think that the intimate fusion of imaginary character and real person in them produces the most unexpected results that are sometimes pure poetry. There is a strange tie between Racine's heroine and the woman of flesh and blood who was making the most outrageous remarks a few minutes before going on stage. I particularly enjoy stories of the theater in which the real suddenly bursts in upon the artificial just as in one of Pirandello's plays.

The other evening, when I was in Rouen to give a lecture, two actors, one old and one young, asked me around to have a drink after the show and we told quite a few of these stories. The young man had been in a recent play (It must have been *Une grande fille tout simple*) in the role of a boy who, disappointed in love, decides on suicide and steals a friend's revolver for the purpose.

The theft is discovered in time and the unfortunate young man is charged with it. In the end the owner of the weapon says severely: "Come on, hand it over!"

Whereupon the young man breaks down and gives up the revolver.

"It was a gripping scene," said my young friend, "but just when I was going to hand over the revolver, I felt in my pockets, and, to my horror, found I'd forgotten to take it on stage. It was lying in the wings."

68

"What a situation! What did you do?"

"For a moment I was absolutely terrified. Then suddenly I had an inspiration, and, with a noble gesture, said, 'No! I want to keep the revolver as a souvenir, but I give you my solemn promise that I shall never use it.'"

What admirable presence of mind, and it reminds me of the story of Madame Dorval in the romantic tragedy *Antony* by Dumas the elder. You remember it? At the end Adèle d'Hervey's lover stabs her, and when her husband enters, the murderer tells Colonel Hervey: "She resisted me, so I killed her!" One night at Rouen, Bocage, who played *Antony*, was furious (why precisely I forget) either with the manager or the audience and bounded off stage without making the famous reply. Marie Dorval, simulating death, saw Bocage disappear and the colonel enter. Sensing the impending catastrophe, she calmly raised herself on one elbow and said to her husband: "*I* resisted him, so *he* killed me . . ." Thunderous applause. Curtain. The audience had seen nothing wrong.

"The audience," said the old actor, "never sees ANYTHING wrong. You know what the great Simone used to say: 'The audience doesn't listen; when it listens, it doesn't hear; when it hears it doesn't understand.'"

"In the theater," I said, "the most unlikely things certainly do get by. Yolande Laffon told me that once at the Théâtre des Arts she acted the part of one Judith in *Éblouissement*, who at a certain moment hurls herself into a burning house. A few minutes later another character comes on to say: 'Judith is dead!' One night the cues got muddled and this actor came on much too soon to tell Judith herself: 'Judith is dead!' Yolande Laffon thought all was lost. But there was not the slightest reaction, the play went on, no one had noticed and not a single spectator made the slightest allusion to it in the intermission. There's the sort of reprieve you get in the theater."

These were the pattern for a whole string of stories. They are interminable. *Adieu.*

The Magic in Marriage

Today I have had the sort of Sunday that I really enjoy, one free from engagements. Beneath my windows the chestnuts are in bud and the most advanced —the one which gives the signal for their rebirth, each spring, is already soft and green. Families are taking their walks at the gentle Sunday pace dictated by their prams. The telephone is silent and I know that I have twelve hours' peace before me. It is wonderful.

I open a book intent on calmly enjoying it for I used to know the author, a sweet-tempered, melancholy and beautiful woman. Her thought held every nice shade of meaning. I had known that she and her husband lived their lives in a great and unstrained solitude, and so I was not surprised to find her slim volume was called *Échos du Silence.* How true it is that silence, like an unseen wall, re-echoes our inmost thoughts.

Those of Camille Belguise remind me of Joubert, and Chardonne, and sometimes of Sainte-Beuve in one of his gentler and more perceptive moods. She has some ad-

70

mirable things to say on human nature and love: "He who loves, projects his own inner image upon the other person and waits to see its reflection. In true love one is two people and you must learn to prefer the other." Yes, not only accept, but prefer the other. "It is a sad business to feel your love waning, for is not loving always cherishing more and more the person who deserves it less and less?"

Camille Belguise does not grant (and I am of her opinion) that love and marriage are dissociated. "But," she says, "What we call love is that magic of marriage which demands that love should fill every moment and which moves so strongly towards a higher plane that when it is frustrated we feel its check like a stab of pain."

And then (for half my Sunday's pleasure lies in my freedom to idle about like this) I opened a novel by Maurice Toesca: *Simone ou le bonheur conjugal.* The dust jacket carries a reproduction of Rodin's *The Kiss.* A novel? Rather a prose poem, a hymn in praise of perfect marriage. "Friends, in the name of her whom I love, I tell you there is no conflict in love. There is only conflict when love is absent. Joy alone can come from this shared emotion."

Have you noticed how our emotional attitudes bear the same stamp of period as pictures and furniture? In Maupassant's and in Proust's day the novelist showed how love was no more than illusion, deception, jealousy and mental torture. As for marriage, for centuries it has been the chief butt of comedy. But now, after years in the wilderness, it has made its comeback. The religious revival has had a share, but so has the earnestness of a generation which has been so sorely tried. In the storm a fixed and solid anchor is essential. What better than a

71

steady love, the complete fusion of two beings? And is not marriage, as Alain says, "the only knot that time draws tighter?"

This is what Toesca's hero discovers as have so many of his contemporaries.

Happy marriages are fashionable. You will say, "Tough luck on the novelist. *Symphonie en blanc majeur* is a lovely title, but a difficult book to write." Who knows? There are many shades in white itself. Happiness, like spring, changes its expression every day, and on my peaceful Sunday at home it was delightful. *Adieu.*

The Other Woman

You couldn't see the other woman at first and yet you knew she was there. Sometimes a stream will flow through a field half hidden underground. If you walk by, you will notice that the grass is thicker and taller and, while the soil is hardly soggy, it will still give underfoot. These are only indications but they are not deceptive: water is there. Or else before an illness; there are still no definite symptoms, you go on with your daily routine but all the same a vague feeling of an apparently baseless disquiet warns you of the lurking danger.

"What's the matter with me?" you say, "I don't feel well."

72

Just the same thing happens when your husband begins to be involved with the Other Woman. What's the matter with him? you think. He's a different person. Every evening before he had always given you an account of his day complete in all its particulars (men love to talk about themselves). He would tell his plans for the morrow. Gradually his reports became more obscure. You noticed inexplicable gaps in his timetable. What is more he seemed to realize how flimsy his explanations were. He tried to gloss over some periods: he contradicted himself. You said to yourself: "Now whatever is he trying to hide?"

You thought you understood him after ten years of married life. You knew his interests, business, political and sporting. He cared a little for art but not in the least for literature and music. But now he was only too happy to discuss the latest books. He asked you carelessly: "Have we got Stendhal's novels? I should like to read them again." You knew quite well that he had never read them. Then, having never noticed before what you were wearing, he suddenly asked: "Why don't you ever wear print dresses? They're so pretty." Or else: "Why don't you get your hair cut short? Pony tails are out of fashion." Even in politics he had changed and had become much less severe on advanced opinions. He held some oddly romantic views on love and dismissed marriage cynically. In short he had changed out of all recognition.

Soon you were quite certain. An underground stream flowed beneath the ground that had once been solid. The Other Woman was there. Who was she? You tried to imagine, building up a picture from the scraps of information your husband brought home to you each evening in spite of himself. She must be young and pretty and beautifully dressed: she was cultured or pretended to be: she rode (for your husband who had not been on a horse for years, said, "My doctor tells me I need more exercise: I'd like to take up riding again.") Almost certainly she lived near the Luxembourg. He was always finding the most unlikely things he simply *had* to do in that district.

And then one day, when you were dining out with friends, you discovered who she was. Not that it was very hard or particularly clever to find *that* out. Unfortunately you had only to watch your husband's face. His eyes caressed her. He pretended to say hardly a word to her, but you noticed the exchange of winks and half smiles which they thought unnoticed and they hurt you. Your hostess told you that it was the Other Woman who had wanted to meet you.

"But why?"

"She'd heard people talk about you and she is just dying to know you."

But from her cheerfully noncommittal tone of voice you knew that she knew. At one and the same time you were upset, unhappy and astounded. In the first place because this woman dared to make advances towards *your* husband. Unconsciously you had come to think that he belonged to you, was a part of you. Unlike many others he was not unattached, he was flesh of your flesh. The Other Woman had as much right to take him from you as she had to cut off your arm or steal your wedding ring.

Astounded, too, because the Other Woman was just as you imagined her and yet somehow different. Of course you had only to listen to her to know where your husband's new ideas and new plans came from, and even his brand-new vocabulary. She talked about horses and races and mentioned the authors of the books in which he had just shown such an unaccustomed interest. But you did not think her either younger or, to be quite frank more beautiful than yourself. Perhaps her forehead *was* fine and her eyes, too, but that was all. Her mouth was greedy and vulgar. She talked with more animation than intelligence and she quickly bored you. "But what can he see in her?" you asked yourself.

When you got home you took the bull by the horns.

"Who one earth were those two? Wherever did you meet them?"

He muttered something about "business acquaintance" and tried to change the subject, but you were bent on nagging him.

"I don't like the woman. She seems to have an awfully good opinion of herself. Why I can't think."

He wanted to contain himself but his feelings were so strong that he contradicted you.

"I don't agree," he answered, trying to adopt a disinterested attitude. "She's pretty and very attractive."

"Pretty! Have you seen her mouth?"

He shrugged his shoulders angrily and answered with a tone of fatuous self-satisfaction.

"Yes, I *have* seen her mouth."

In your fury you continued (as you thought) to pull the Other Woman to pieces. Neither you nor your husband went to sleep until after 2 A.M. after an exhausting and painful scene. The next morning he was extremely icy and told you.

"I shan't be lunching here today."

"Why?"

"Because I shan't be lunching here. That's all! I presume that I am still capable of managing my own affairs?"

It was then that you realized that the night before you had made a dangerous mistake. You don't get a man away from a woman he loves by running her down. In his eyes she is adorable: if you say she isn't, he will think not that he is wrong but that you can't see or rather won't see that she is because you are madly jealous. We will speak of this again. *Adieu.*

The Other Woman SECOND LETTER

Being a sensible woman you clearly saw the risk you ran. Of course your natural reaction would have been to make their lives a burden to them. You could have followed your husband, or had him followed. She had a husband herself who probably had no inkling of what was going on. What then would have been simpler than to warn him and get him to watch her? But, alone with your misery, you thought again.

While I have every right to be jealous and to make their lives a misery, what good will it do me? My husband will only see me as he did last night as an obstacle, the odd person out, perhaps even the shrew. Up to now we have been united in spite of everything by common memories, habits and, I think, affection on his part. He felt guilty and in hurting me he hurt himself. He tried to make up in little acts of tenderness for the love of which he was tempted to cheat me.

Tempted? Only tempted? There's nothing to show he has actually fallen. It can quite easily have gone no further than walks and conversations in bars. If I upset him, if I make him feel that he is tied to me, he will only want to escape. If she is driven in the same direction, who knows where it will all end? If it finishes in our complete separation, I shall have destroyed my own home myself, whereas if I am just the slightest bit patient . . .

Then a new burst of anger carried you away.

All the same it's too unfair! Here am I. I've given my whole life to my husband. Since my marriage I haven't so much as glanced at another man. They might have been so many dummies for all I was concerned. I only bothered about them in so far as they could be useful to my husband's career. But was I right? Didn't I make him feel too sure of me? My friends often told me, "Look out . . . a man needs to be kept dangling. If he stops finding you mysterious he'll only look for mystery somewhere else!" Yet it would have been, it still is, so easy for me to make him jealous. Without doing anything wrong. Just by being a little less cold to other people's husbands.

A lot of his friends have tried and still try to press their attentions on me. "Can I call on you in the evening?" they all ask me. "Can I take you to the theater when Jacques is away on business?" And I've always refused, intimidated by my decision to be completely faithful to him. If I were to accept, it would make him suffer too, and wouldn't that be a way of reminding him that other men still find his wife attractive?

You had enough sense to drop that idea. It was stupid

and risky. Stupid because you cannot go against your-self. In fact you love your husband, however much he may seem to be in the wrong, and you would be hor-rified if his friends pressed their attentions too far. Risky, because you could never foresee how your hus-band would react. If he had reason to fear a sudden in-fatuation on your part, would he be all tears and apolo-gies? Who could tell? If he was really head over heels in love with the Other Woman, he could just as easily go to the opposite extreme and say, "To hell with my wife! I've always made allowances for her, but if she makes no attempt to hold our marriage together, why should I try? Let us each go our own way."

Coquetry is a two-edged weapon and wounds who-ever misuses it. You realized that, but what was to be done? All through your lonely luncheon you meditated sadly.

Is he lunching with her at this very moment? Is he telling her about the row we had last night, and does she seem a refuge of peace, sweetness and happiness in con-trast to my tears and screams? I spoke and thought ill of her: now I'm alone I have to admit that I was biased and unfair. When I judged her, I was her rival, not a reasonable woman. I must try to understand. If I did not fear her as an enemy and a menace to my own happiness, how would she strike me?

You then bravely tried to control your feelings, to look the fact squarely in the face and when your hus-band came in that evening he was surprised—and re-lieved—to find you so calm. You made no effort to find out what he had been doing and it was he himself who volunteered the information, with a touching lack of address, that he had *happened* to meet the Other Woman at an exhibition of paintings. You did not inquire what miracle had dragged him, the least artistic of men, into a gallery! On the contrary you suggested that if he liked the couple, it would be nice to ask them to lunch or dinner. He was quite taken aback and even raised objections.

"Do you think so?" he said, "He's a bore; She's amusing but so different from you. Anyway you said you didn't like her and I wouldn't want to force her down your throat."

You confessed that the night before you were tired and bad-tempered and that really you had nothing against the Other Woman, quite the contrary. By force of arms you gained the battle of the invitation. It was doubly clever. You thought, and rightly so, that by bringing her into your home you would rob her of her attraction as something forbidden and mysterious. And above all you wanted to see her again, to study her, and to try to find out what it was about her that attracted your husband. *Adieu.*

The Other Woman THIRD LETTER

And so the Other Woman came to dinner with you. You received her warmly, you watched her carefully, listened to her closely and tried to put yourself in the position of a casual acquaintance—or of a man in love with her. It was a hard task but useful. You noticed several little things that had escaped you when first you met. After she had left, in the darkness as your husband slept, you drew up the balance sheet for the evening.

She's no prettier than I am, but she makes much better use of her looks. She has plenty of taste. Her beige woolen dress, her narrow red belt, her beret, they were all perfect. She was beautifully turned out. . . . A matter of money? No. Neither the dress nor the beret came from an exclusive shop. The only thing was the love with which they were chosen. It's easy to see she tries to make herself a work of art. And be frank about it, to a great extent she succeeds.

And then on another level I can see why she amuses Jacques. I'm quiet and shy. Except when I'm really angry, or happy and forget myself, I seldom put my feelings into words. It isn't my fault. My parents brought me up very strictly. I look stiff, I am stiff. The Other Woman is naturalness itself. In front of her my husband quoted a remark by Stendhal (Jacques quoting Stendhal, it's alarming . . . and funny!) It was: I like naturalness so much that I stop in the street to watch a dog gnawing a bone! She said, "That's awfully good!" She takes an obvious pleasure in food and drink. She talks so well about fruit and flowers. The sensual has its charms. I noticed that when I watched her. She tells a good story and she never lets the conversation flag while I always have to look for something to say.

When you were alone again you cried, no longer from hatred or even from jealousy, rather from humility. All of a sudden you felt unworthy of your husband. You came to think: He's only gone to a more striking and more lovable woman: is that a crime? With you an hour's tears always bring a crisis to a wholesome end. In an instant you were on your feet and drying your eyes. You had just decided to beat the Other Woman at her own game. Her gaiety was attractive? You would be gay. Her conversation was seductive? You would nurse yours by reading and meeting interesting people. She had filled your husband's life with art exhibitions and films? Was that not within the reach of any woman, particularly yourself?

You will long remember the dreadful time that ensued. With the Other Woman triumphant, you had decided to be the Other Woman. Oh how wretched you made yourself for those three months. And how you deserved to succeed. You flung yourself heart and soul into the battle. You remember what a wretched failure it was? Courageously you played your tragi-comedy. You pretended to be light-hearted when really you were in despair. You suggested to your husband all sorts of amusements for your Saturdays and Sundays which you thought well chosen, yet at first he merely raised his eyebrows. "What's the matter with you?" he said. "You're crazy. On Sunday all I want is peace and quiet and now you want to drag me round the museums . . . . No, thank you!" And then another day: "Why have you become such a chatter-box? You talk, talk, talk, you just can't be silenced. Honestly, you get on my nerves."

And how you cried that day when, having carefully selected a suit of which the Other Woman, you were sure, would have approved, you proudly presented your-self to your husband who noticed nothing at first. In the end you asked him: "Jacques, you haven't said a word. . . . What do you think of my new suit?"

"Oh," he answered, "not bad."

81

At that moment you thought all was lost. The only thing to do was to throw in the towel and leave the field to the Other Woman. The example of the Third Woman saved you by showing you where you had gone wrong.

Annabelle was your childhood friend. Even at that age her complete lack of character astonished you. A good-natured girl, too good-natured, she was everybody's slave: particularly yours. Once upon a time Annabelle tried to be like you. She copied the way you did your hair, even the way you did your lessons. Later on when you met her again, you found that she was just as ready to follow the most convenient model. Did her boy friends admire some pretty blonde? She had her hair dyed. Did she see some film star with a short nose divinely shaped as though by some master sculptor? She wanted a nose just like it and went running off to a plastic surgeon. Chance set her in your path just when you were most desperate. You saw how ill the perfect nose and platinum hair became the wretched girl. It was like a flash of inspiration.

"What I need," you said to yourself, "is not *naturalness* but *my* naturalness."

From that moment you gave up trying to be the Other Woman. You set about making her your friend and you succeeded easily enough. Unknown to yourself you carried a lot of prestige with her. Your husband was always telling her of your virtues: he appreciated them even more than you thought. Once you tried to draw her to you she came and not without bringing some odd changes in her wake.

Finding her at home when he came back from the office, your husband got used to seeing her, no longer as the heroine of a novel, but as a piece of drawing room furniture. At first your unexpected friendship amused him. He felt he was the triumphant pasha lording it over two women. But very soon relations between you and the Other Woman became much closer than between the Other Woman and your husband. A woman speaks more freely to another woman. And because she was talkative, she was imprudent and went so far as to tell you what she thought were your husband's faults and to add that she valued your friendship far more than his infatuation. You were sensible enough not to tell this to your Jacques, it would only have hurt him and wounded his pride. This would not only have been spite but bad tactics into the bargain. He wouldn't have believed you: he would have complained to the Other Woman and she, of course, would have denied the whole story.

Patiently you let things develop. In one particular alone you took the Other Woman's advice and made use of her experience. She gave you the invaluable names of dressmakers and hairdressers from whom you sought, not to imitate her style but to discover your own. Like her you aimed at perfection and hit *your* perfection. Bursting with a joy that was indescribable, you saw your husband's eyes rest appreciatively upon you and noticed how proud he seemed to be to go out with you now.

As for the Other Woman, you had drawn her to you and you went on inviting her with real heroism. You had to wear out her prestige. It didn't take long. She ran out of stories, and began repeating herself. Did she go on meeting your husband away from you? Even that became unlikely, for now he had stopped lying about his day's activities. Your triumph was splendid — and secret — when, on your suggestion that you and he should ask the Other Woman and her husband to join you on a motoring holiday, your husband had angrily burst out:

"That woman again! I can't see why you're so keen on her."

"But don't you think she's nice?"

"Nice," he grumbled, "nice. Just because you like a good wine, it's no reason why you should drink it with every meal. . . . And anyway frankly I'd rather be alone with you."

Little by little after that the Other Woman vanished from your life. There were gaps between your meetings and the gaps grew wider. The Other Woman was only a shadow; then she ceased to exist.

Your marriage was saved. *Adieu*.

Choosing Books

My soul's Unknown, you ask me what books you should read. My reply will no doubt surprise you, but follow it in spite of this. My master Alain used to say that one should be a man (or a woman) of few books and proved the excellence of this principle by his own practice. To all intents and purposes his library was composed of a few great authors: Homer, Horace, Tacitus, Saint-Simon, Retz, Rousseau, the Mémorial, Stendhal, Balzac, George Sand, Victor Hugo and of course the philosophers: Plato, Aristotle, Descartes, Spinoza,

Kant, Hegel, and Auguste Comte. In the course of his life he added Romain Rolland, Valéry, Claudel, Proust and Kipling as well.

It was a severely restricted choice, but he knew every word of those great works. He read them over and over again and with each reading discovered fresh beauties in them. He considered that no one really knows an author unless he is able to go straight to the page he wants. In which of Balzac's novels does Vautrin first meet Rubempré: in which do we discover that Félix de Vandenesse has got married? Which volume of Proust shows the first appearance of Vinteuil's septet? If you cannot answer, you are not a real reader. "The important thing," said Valéry, "is not just to find, but to absorb what you find." A woman who has absorbed a few great works has far more culture that she who skims through three new books a day.

Should one then refuse to read contemporary writers? Obviously not, and in any case from their ranks will come the classics of tomorrow. But one must guard against a lack of discrimination. How? In the first place by giving the year's vintage time to mature. So many books which were hailed as masterpieces by their publishers or by a literary clique will be forgotten in six months' time. We should not burden our minds with them. Rather wait, scrutinize them as they pass and choose those we want for friends. Among our contemporaries each one of us has his chosen authors and it is their work which he should follow. I read every published word written by a few young authors whom I trust. I should be glad to find others, but I would not want them to be too many—I should be submerged.

As soon as we are satisfied as to a book's intellectual and

85

aesthetic worth, we must buy it. Only by actually pos-
sessing a book can we know it through and through. For
our first meeting with an author it is legitimate and even
reasonable to have recourse to borrowing. Once we have
decided to adopt him, he must have the right of domicile.
We marry the woman and buy the books with which we
want to live.

How then should one read? If a book enthralls us our
first reading will be swift and enraptured, but our subse-
quent readings (and a good book will be reread a hundred times) should be made with pencil in hand. Nothing is better calculated to form our good taste than
copying out particularly distinguished passages and
noting down any deep thoughts. You must promise to
read every word of the authors you admire. The person
who skips a single one of Balzac's long descriptions of
towns or houses is no true *balzacien*.

One effective method of reading is to branch out from
a central subject, one book bringing another in its train.
For example I read and admire Proust, and from my
reading of his work I find that he admired Ruskin and
George Sand. What a reader of his quality found good
cannot be without merit. In the same way Chateaubriand
acquainted me with Joubert: Charles du Bos made me
read *Eurydice deux fois perdue* and Maurice Baring
initiated me into Chekov and Gogol. In this way we form
links in a chain of intellectual friendship. It is up to you
to take your place in it. *Adieu*.

Advice to a Young Lady Unable to Sleep

I write to you with the pad on my knees in the train between Marseilles and Nice. The sky is a brilliant, cloudless blue. The little walled towns with their paved streets have taken refuge in the hilltops to protect themselves from the Saracens. The rocky golden crags have a clarity of definition which you find only in Greece or Provence. The scenery is simply glorious, but the two men with whom I share the carriage cast not so much as a glance outside. Pencil in hand, foreheads creased, they are completely absorbed in their crossword puzzles.

"Perhaps it will never happen," murmurs one.

"Uncertain," answers the other.

"Yes! It fits!" says the first man happily.

I watch them, slightly astonished at their purposeless concentration. But I am the one who is wrong. Newspapers in their wisdom offer their readers crossword puzzles for the very same reason that the Church in her infinite prudence imposes the rosary on the faithful. They are both excellent means of removing one's obsessions and ending that appalling meditation on oneself which is the worst of tortures.

My fair Unknown, you and I, all of us have known those terrible obsessions which buzz round and round in one's mind annihilating every other thought. They can be prompted by a number of things. Your husband may have had a row with you and still seem very bad-tempered; you may have yielded to a stupid temptation and now be unable to pay for what you have bought: a cruelly wounding remark about yourself may have been passed on to you, and you discover that the woman who made it was someone you had always thought your friend. Perhaps none of this is tragedy; in a month's time you will think how exaggerated your reactions were, but it is now. Your obsession gnaws your brain and literally makes you ill. You must have a remedy.

Where can you find one? Unfortunately your will does not completely control your thoughts and you vainly tell yourself to forget all about it. Back buzzes the nagging thought like a mosquito. In any case you cannot drive it away by direct action, you can only lull it to sleep indirectly by filling your mind with other thoughts. Crossword puzzles, bridge, canasta, knitting are all occupations which demand concentrated attention, and anything to do is a remedy. When you are obsessed, you must cheat your brain by always keeping it busy. Gradually the hateful vibration will weaken and finally it will disappear. Time conquers any thought. A little patience, a little perseverance and something will overcome it. Crosswords, I thank you.

One danger remains — nighttime. I see you in your bed, flopping about like a fish out of water, vainly trying to get to sleep. In the dark the obsession becomes a ghost. This is the time when remedies are less helpful. A book? You will still have to be able to follow what you read. . . . Shut your eyes and count sheep? That may work with Englishmen . . . or perhaps with shepherds.

For my part I have three recipes. The first is to picture to myself scenes from my childhood or youth. They eliminate my obsession because I am recreating a period of time long before the events which gave it birth. It is crowded out. But you need to be strong-willed to keep your attention riveted on those scenes.

The second method: watch the spots of light which always form under your closed eyelids and try to turn them into people or things. They will gradually turn into dreams and away you go.

The third method, the simplest, is to ask your doctor for something to make you sleep. Sleeping pills are far less dangerous than insomnia. In short never let an obsession dominate your mind. It will drive you mad.

And that would be a pity. *Adieu.*

Optimism

Querida, you reproach me for being an optimist. You are right, I do tend to think that things work out in the end. "If you fell off a precipice," one of my army friends told me in the war, "you'd probably think the bottom was well padded and so you wouldn't worry until you landed."

That is an exaggeration! Unlike Voltaire's Pangloss I do not believe that all is for the best in the best of worlds. Life can be hard and horrible: I know it because I have experienced it myself. But: in the first place I do not believe that life is entirely evil: far from it. I refuse to consider the human lot as "terrible." It is true that it is odd; it is true that we revolve on a blob of earth in infinite space without any great idea why we are here,

89

and it is true that we are bound to die. Those are the facts of our position and we must face them courageously. I agree that we revolve on a blob of earth. There is one question and one alone, being on that blob of earth what can we and what ought we to do?

In the second place I am an optimist in the sense that I hold it possible for us to do something to better our own lives and the lives of the human race in general. I believe that we have made enormous progress. Man has to a great degree tamed Nature. His material empire is infinitely greater than it was. The Pessimist will reply, "Yes, but all man's wonderful inventions are used only for war, and in the end humanity will be responsible for its own destruction." I do not think that necessarily follows. It depends in part upon ourselves and my optimism springs from my belief in human nature. I know the nobility of that nature, and I know that one can call the best out of everyone. In short it is better to speak to man of his liberty than of his servitude.

In the third place I realize that my natural reaction to any given event is to look on the bright rather than the dark side of it. For example, circumstances have put me in the bad graces of someone influential. The Pessimist would think, How disastrous. My career is bound to suffer. I say, "What luck! Thank God I've got that fool off my hands." Such is the nature of my comparative optimism. I followed the example of Alain, and we vowed that we would be optimists, because, unless invincible optimism is your rule, events begin to justify the blackest pessimism. For despair and any other state of depression into which a man lets himself fall, breed misery and frustration. If I think that I am going to fall, fall I shall. This is called vertigo and peoples are just as liable to it as individuals. If I think I cannot serve my country, I cannot. *Within the natural order I am the storm and the sunshine: first in myself and then to those around me.* Pessimism is catching. If I believe my neighbor dishonest, and if I show him I distrust him, I will make him distrustful and dishonest. The secret of the wisdom of antiquity was to teach hope and not fear. Our wise men have changed all that, they teach despair, but I do not think them very wise.

"Look," the Pessimist tells me. "You really think your belief in mankind, in life itself is a piece of wisdom. Hasn't it brought you some awful disillusionments? In the ceaseless battle of life has it not been to you a source of weakness? Have you not given scope to evil by long refusing to recognize it as such?" Yes, I admit that I have been bitterly disillusioned. The war years in particular, with the horrors of Nazism and the bloody ditch separating two halves of my country, with exile, the arrest of my family, the plunder of my home, and the desertion of my friends in moments of danger, have given me ample grounds for doubting the perfection of this universe of ours.

But why? I have never believed it perfect. I have always known that there were wicked men (who incidentally are nearly always foolish or miserable), and I have always known that in times of disaster the masses become stupid and blood-thirsty. My optimism has always consisted, and it still consists today, of this and this alone; I believe that we can influence events to a certain extent and that even if, in spite of all our efforts, we must suffer misfortune, we can still overcome it by the way in which we endure it. Descartes has expressed my feelings far better than I can ever do. "My principle has ever been to attempt to overcome myself rather than fortune and to change my desires rather than the natural order." To love the good in people around me, to avoid the wicked, to enjoy my good fortune and to bear my ill, and to remember to forget, that has been my optimism. It has helped me to live; may it help you, too. . . . *Adieu.*

Woman and Society

Some hundred years ago George Sand, a woman of genius of whom you are not very fond, was bravely fighting for the emancipation of women. But let there be no mistake, the measures George Sand proposed then would be far from satisfying women now. Sand was not concerned with the political equality of the sexes, which she held to be neither practicable nor desirable. What she demanded above all else was their sexual equality.

What did she mean by that? Simply that a woman should never be forced into a loveless surrender of her body. Without full consent, Sand considered physical union criminal and sacrilegious even within the married state. "Woman should have the right to withdraw from it. I believe and proclaim that one ought either to love with one's whole being or else live in absolute chastity." In her eyes the sin lay not in leaving a lover for someone you really love, but in giving yourself to somebody you do not love, albeit that person is your husband. But men did not admit of sexual equality. "Women are treated as whores in love," wrote Sand, "and as servants in marriage. They are unloved, they are merely used, and in spite of this you hope to subject them to the law of fidelity."

How, she asked, can you justify demanding from woman a standard of fidelity which a man would consider pointless and absurd were it applied to himself? Why should the wife remain chaste if her husband is coarse, loose-living and promiscuous? The answer might well have been that many wives remain neither chaste nor faithful. But the injustice lay in this; such women were treated as criminals, adultery by the wife was punishable with imprisonment, the adulterous mother was dishonored in her children's eyes, whereas the gay Lothario ranked in popular judgment with the drunkard or the glutton, and was dismissed with the same indulgent smile bordering on complicity. The sexual inequality, she thought, made it difficult for an intelligent and refined woman to find happiness either in free love or in marriage.

George Sand's other demand was for economic equality for both sexes. In those days a married woman had no free control either of her income or her possessions. As an unmarried girl, George Sand (or rather Aurore Dupin) had been the owner of the estate at Nohant bequeathed her by her grandmother. Once she was married she had had to resign the management to her husband and he had set it on the road to ruin. Every husband had this absolute power over the couple's joint wealth. Marriage placed the wife, even after her majority, in a state of perpetual minority, and since divorce was nonexistent, it was extremely difficult for her to free herself from the toils. George Sand demanded for the

93

wife as for the husband, the same freedom to dissolve a marriage and to control an income. Such were the bounds of her feminism. She did not envisage political actions; that is not to say she was without political ideals—in fact she was an ardent republican and socialist; but merely that she did not assert woman's right or eligibility to vote. We can see now that she was mistaken on this point, for it is precisely through political equality that women have gradually achieved economic equality. Once women had the vote, candidates, depending upon their support, became more respectful of their wishes and of their rights.

Nevertheless, the sphere of morals is practically untouched. Today one half of mankind lives in a sort of slavery, since countless women, though they may color their compulsion with myth and ceremony, accept the sale of their bodies as the price of survival. The lawgiver is, to all intents and purposes, powerless in the face of the servile attitude of the mind. The emancipation of women will be a task for women themselves, not from man's tyranny, but from the ideas they have built up of men and of their own nature.

"The sexes" said the poet Rilke, "are more closely related than perhaps we imagine and the world's great revival will certainly arise from this factor: men and women, freed from their errors, will no longer seek in each other their opposites. As human beings they will unite to bear together firmly and patiently, the burdens that the infirmity of the flesh has laid upon them. The day will come when the girl—and the woman—will find her real being, and the words "girl" and "woman" will no longer describe the opposite of male, but something separate and having its own validity: In no sense the complement, but a complete form of life, woman in her true humanity." When that day dawns, it will see the emancipation not only of women but of men as well, for the tyrant is always the slave. *Adieu.*

Carpe Diem

Querida, in the sunshine of Monte Carlo I have just been reading Paul Valéry's *Lettres à quelques uns,* recently published by his family. Do you like Valéry? I hope so. The opposite would give us grounds for serious disagreement. I consider Valéry to be one of the most intelligent men I have ever known, the other being Alain, the philosopher. That will put the cat among the pigeons!

In one of his letters Valéry writes: "The story of a sensitive person can be condensed to this: the older he grows the more he regrets not having had the things that once repelled him. At one point—very early on—women aroused feelings almost of repulsion in him. Love seemed an obscenity to him. Later the very idea of money, and the men and things connected with it, was repugnant. At some stage success—even glory appeared to him as shame. But what he retains—the essence distilled from all these by-products—is so delicate, so light, so slight and so priceless a thing that there is never enough of it to perfume a whole lifetime. Then his mind travels back, and he is left with his regrets, the stupid smirk of the man who is misunderstood, and the bitter taste of his own bitterness."

There is much truth in these reflections, dating from 1915, before Valéry, in his turn, tasted glory and its by-products. It is madness to refuse what one is offered when one can honorably accept it. Yes, if we are to avoid outbursts of baffled rage against ourselves when we reach the age when love is no longer at our beck and call, we must love when we are young, and, yes, if our old age is not to be miserable and embittered, we must achieve something to make it honored. Success in itself is no proof of genius, but too late it frees genius from the temptation of chasing success. *Moral*: we should never despise what can be gained without doing anything despicable.

Now, my dear, when you have a grown-up son, warn him against absolute and abstract principles which bring a thwarted old age in their train. Tell him to lay up happy memories for himself by loving well. Gérard Bauer, who is here with me and who is at this very moment writing a preface to the *Memoirs of Casanova*, was talking to me yesterday about this astounding adventurer who could not meet a girl without seducing her or pass a gaming table without plunging into the play. What happened to him? In his ripe old age, sought-after for the charm of his conversations, he wrote his tempestuous life story and stepped straight into immortality. That does not mean, however, that your son should take Casanova as an example. In any case one has to be singularly gifted to play so very robust a role and we are not in the eighteenth century! I would merely offer him the wisdom of Horace: "Seize the day—the girl—the fortune—if the gods give you the chance."

I am well aware that serenity, and freedom from envy, desire, and ambition, are the best attributes of old age and I know men who have achieved happiness without having possessed any of the things others deem vital to it. I myself try to accept my life for what it is, without comparing it with others. I succeed, but I am only too well aware that this philosophic state would be infinitely harder of achievement had this life of mine brought me nothing. In short we should never be indecently anxious to pursue the good things of this world, but should welcome them if we meet them on our way. Few are they who have never had the chance to make their happiness and fewer those who have taken that chance. Having found you, my dear, I take and keep you. *Adieu.*

The Different Ways of Pleasing

Men have existed for six thousand years and the creatures most concerned with them, their women, have been forced to try to please them, many of them by correcting, with much ingenuity, either nature's deficiencies or the ravages of time. But until our own day you could still see another, larger, group of women who made no attempt to change their lot. Were they ugly? Very well then, they remained ugly. Did no one love them? So be it, they put aside any thought of love. Did they age more rapidly than their husbands? That was their misfortune. Balzac's novels are full of resigned wives, who at the ripe old age of thirty or forty, have given up the struggle while their husbands turn to some younger woman. Between 1900 and 1930 there were innumerable Frenchwomen, in Paris as often as in the provinces, who had renounced all hope. It is true that they were still the hardworking mistresses of their houses and mothers of their children, but they no longer were, nor even wished to be, in the full sense, wives. They dressed and did their hair just well enough to satisfy the proprieties: indeed they would have felt guilty if they had spent time and money on their personal appearance which they would otherwise have been able to devote to charity, their homes, or their children.

The last fifty and more particularly the last twenty years, have changed all that. Here and there we may still chance to meet a female of this vanished species, an ageless, shapeless monster, but such encounters have become very rare. Look at the women in the streets of any small industrial or market town. Nearly all the younger ones are tastefully dressed, their hair "permanented." In the large towns this is a matter of course, and the girl who struggles on a small salary would far rather forego her food than her regular visit to the hair-dresser.

What has caused this vast change of attitude? I think the films have exerted an enormous influence by offering all classes, first of all, types of beauty which they have been forced to copy, and then love stories which show the use to which women can put this beauty. Film stars have taken the parts once played among the Greeks by the goddesses of Olympus. They have been the models: they have also made men more demanding.

Women's magazines too have guided their readers and have proved that if beauty is not within the reach of all, grace and charm are, if they will only take the trouble. The influence of America, where Youth and Beauty have become the most exacting of divinities, has hastened this moral transformation. In addition the bonds of marriage are no longer indissoluble, and hence the married woman must still defend her position, while the unmarried woman's hopes are higher than they once were, with class distinction less marked and the field for conquest correspondingly wider. Ample reason for a woman not to neglect her personal appearance. And yet. . . .

And yet there are still women who say, "Me? Oh the latest fashions don't worry me nor how other people think I look! I dress any old how, to suit myself not to please you!" That is what they say, granted, but is it what they think? The truth is, I imagine, that they, like everyone else, have an ideal image of themselves. Only it is a different image.

For example the outdoor girl has all the freshness of youth, and she wants her appearance to suggest health and freedom. She knows how well she looks in gray flannels and a sweater molded to her athletic figure. So you will see her most of the day carelessly dressed like this, with her hair a little untidy and her cheeks owing their color to nothing except fresh air and exercise. But that does not mean that she takes no pains with her dress. On the contrary it means that she realizes that that *particular* style of dress suits her. You can be sure that her sweater has been most carefully chosen to match her complexion and that the apparent untidiness of her hair has been cunningly achieved by the "windswept" cut, while that healthy tan is not due purely and simply to sunshine.

Watch the women who "don't care what impression they make on the rest of the world" when at last they have met a man they want to attract. You see a sudden transformation. You can tell the woman is in love by the very fact that she pays more attention to her dress. "What's the matter with Dominique?" say her friends. "She's become almost pretty." She feels she should defend her abrupt change of style. "I don't like lipstick," she says, "but what can I do? When every woman wears it, you look like a ghost if you don't. I didn't want to get myself a new hat this year, things are so ridiculously expensive, but the fashions have changed so much that I gave myself quite a shock when I saw myself in the glass with my old hat on. I'd given up having permanents, but when all's said and done it is more economical." Don't apologize, Dominique, your heart has its own good reasons: you are passing through a natural phase, and now you take an interest in your own appearance because you want someone to take an interest in you.

To be attractive is a virtue and you know it. *Adieu.*

After Seeing Oedipus Rex

I saw you in the distance, the other night, *Querida*, at the Comédie Français. You were wearing a pleated white dress and a golden girdle that gave you an air of the ill-fated King of Thebes, for the company was performing the *Oedipus Rex* of Sophocles. I was touched to remember that it was in the same Salle Richelieu that I saw you for the first time. You were very lovely.

The tragedy did not upset your calm. That is as it should be; a good play does not shatter its spectators. The emotions it arouses are channeled by its poetry and soothed by the sense of destiny. Why worry about an outcome which you already know? Before you ever sat down you knew that Oedipus would gouge his eyes out with a golden pin and that Jocasta would hang herself. And so you merely patted your hair and smiled at the man beside you.

The comments of my neighbors surprised me:

"What perfect melodrama!"

"What a thriller!"

"It's pure Simenon: *The Snow was Black.*"

A lady of a certain age ("Why" said Byron, "are there mature women?") was asking:

"But why does the fool press on with it? In the first ten minutes everyone knows what he's going to find. Now it was plain enough to Jocasta that things should be left alone. Women have intuition. They can turn a blind eye to the unpleasant. But this conceited male has to get to the bottom of the whole thing. It serves him right!"

But the truth is that Oedipus, as Sophocles conceived him, is bound to act as he does. From all eternity Destiny has shaped his slightest gesture and his lightest word. "It is Fate!" as they say in the *Belle Hélène* and therein, I think, lies the great difference between ourselves and the Greeks. I think that man can *make* his destiny in spite of the gods. Sophocles did not believe this. His belief was the source of drama of great beauty and lives of great tragedy. For, although Oedipus had only fulfilled the words of the oracle, he nevertheless felt that he was guilty and deserved all his punishment. "It was written that I should kill my father and marry my mother, and therefore I must be punished." It is the harsh morality of a Calvin or a Jansen.

A point which you and I share with the Greeks is our feeling that incest is unnatural. This is the most enduring of all primitive taboos, at all events with regard to direct lineal descent. In the collateral line the Pharaohs ignored it and Byron took a twisted, gloomy pleasure in defying it. When I was writing his life, I had to make delicate inquiries about this very point. There were many English scholars who denied that Byron and Augusta Leigh had, in fact, been in such guilty relationship. At last his grandson's widow (she was eighty-five) opened the secret archives for me. By the light of a pair of candles I spent a most moving night deciphering the letters and private diaries. By morning I knew the truth, and, feeling rather embarrassed, I went to see my aged hostess.

"Lady Lovelace," I said, "I fear there can be no further question . . . I have found definite proof of incest. As a conscientious historian I shall have to interpret the facts in the light of these documents. I am sorry."

She looked at me in surprise.

"Why apologize?" she asked. "Byron and Augusta? Of course! Did you really have any doubts about it? Why? There they were, two young people snowbound in that gloomy old house for weeks on end. . . . What else could they do?"

Which showed me that the taboo was weaker in nineteenth-century England than it was in ancient

Greece. However I still think it has its use in preserving peace in the family—and in the heart. Go to see *Jocaste* ... *Phèdre* and *Le Feu sur la Terre* but keep your love affairs outside the family circle. *Adieu.*

The Limits of One's Patience

Some men are strongly tempted to be generous to the point of weakness. Because their imaginations are so lively, they foresee the happiness which will spring from a concession they may make, and the sorrow refusal would entail: they appreciate the deep-seated motives that excuse some sudden whim or outburst of anger which another would have blamed severely. "To understand all is to pardon all." These excellent people go from pardon to pardon and from sacrifice to sacrifice.

Their conduct would be saintly if it were only themselves whom they sacrificed. But men are not made to live with saints, and tolerance becomes a sin when it spoils dangerously those who are its object. The over-affectionate husband, and the father who is too lenient, against his will and unknown to himself, conditions his wife and children to believe that their wishes will encounter no resistance, however far they go. But this does not square with life as we live it. When these victims of kindness run up against the hard facts of life (as some day they must), they will take them badly, much worse than those who are not mollycoddled. They will

103

try to use the tears, and complaints, the melancholy and sickness, the weapons which have hitherto proved successful. They will dash themselves against indifference or mockery and they will despair. Many a failure has been due to this and this alone.

The members of any household or family must feel they are loved and that the other members are prepared to bear with them, but that there are bounds, too, to that forbearance and that once these have been passed, the culprit will be left to his own devices. To act otherwise is only to cultivate the seeds of his own disaster and to place him in an untenable position. To undertake to pay the debts of a gambler or a wastrel will only ruin you without either helping or curing the man you are trying to save. By marrying a woman you pity, but do not love, you only store up unhappiness for yourself and for her too. "Brothers, let us be hard," said the great Nietzsche. If we change it to: "Brothers, let us know how to be hard if necessary," it will be less well-phrased but much truer to life.

What I have just said is naturally applicable to nations too. In the family of nations there are peoples who are too kind. As in the family sphere so also in the international. "To understand all is to forgive all" is a dangerous maxim. The cause of peace is not served by tolerating acts which are already acts of war. There, too, the bounds should be firmly set. Peoples, like individuals, demand and exact for just as long as they meet no resistance. Forces are balanced when the reaction equals the action. If the reaction is nil, balance is impossible.

Now you know what awaits you. To you I am kind and indulgent. I can be severe should you ever deserve it. *Adieu.*

Cleopatra's Nose

"Had Cleopatra's nose been shorter the whole history of the world would have been different." When we examine the course either of our own lives, or of the history of our own country, we are often tempted to apply Pascal's remark to ourselves. Such terrible tragedies have grown from incidents so inconsiderable and from such bewildering coincidences that we, in our innocence, wonder at the haphazardness of Fate.

If Arlette Stavisky had not been so fond of jewelry, the history of the Third Republic would have been different. If the soldiers who brought Napoleon the cannon in the nick of time in Vendémiaire had stopped ten minutes for a drink, they would have wiped Austerlitz and Wagram from the history books. If President Wilson had brought a Republican Senator with him to Paris, America would for fifty years, perhaps forever, have participated in the political life of Europe.

Once we start reflecting on the past we cannot avoid such thoughts. "If I had not decided to go to Saint-Tropez for my Easter holidays that year, I should never have met that woman who made me so unhappy." The truth of such an argument is not evident. Undoubtedly unforeseen events do continually alter the course of our adventures, but it would have taken a series of quite extraordinary coincidences to turn it in entirely the opposite direction.

If you had not gone to Saint-Tropez you would have gone to Saint-Raphaël, and there you would have met another woman of the same type. She would have attracted you as strongly as the first for just the same reason; because unwittingly at that moment you were in search of suffering of this sort. The minor events of your life would have been very different, but the overall pattern would have remained practically the same.

Lord Dunsany has written a curious play on this theme. In the first act we see a man miss his train. The gates close just as he reaches the platform. This seems to be the reason for his failure in life, and he is always saying: "Just think, if I had only been one second earlier." Then one day an eastern peddler offers him a magic crystal which allows its owner to transform at his pleasure *one* of the events in his past. Of course the hero chooses to arrive on the platform one second earlier. This time he passes the gates, catches the train and his life begins anew. But in different circumstances it is just as much a failure as the first, for the motives for that failure lay not in outside events, but in his own character.

The same is true of the lives of nations. They do not escape their inherent doom. If the gunners of the Vendémiaire had come too late, Bonaparte's life would for a time have been changed, yet that of France would in its essentials have remained the same. Another Bonaparte would have arisen. Each generation carries a certain body of heroes and men of action. But in peaceful eras these heroes remain unemployed. The Bonapartes of 1895 died in some garrison town in the provinces, kings of their own household, lawgivers to their battalions. Had Cleopatra's nose been shorter, Rome would nonetheless have known her successive grandeur and decay.

Had your nose been longer, my dear, I should none-theless be writing this letter to an Unknown. Only it would have been another Unknown. *Adieu.*

The Chronophage

Chronophage: the word was coined, I think by Montherlant. It describes a dangerous breed in the human species: time devourers.

The chronophage is generally a man who has very little to do himself, and not knowing what to make of the time on his hands decides to fill it by devouring yours. The audacity of the animal passes all belief. He writes to authors he has never met asking for a reply by return. He carries his cruelty so far as to enclose a stamped and addressed envelope, to the profound embarrassment of the honest letter writer. He asks for a perfectly useless appointment, and if you are so unfortunate as to grant his request he clings to you like a limpet until exasperation gets the better of his host's politeness. He tells you the story of his life and asks you all about your own. You are more than fortunate if he does not keep a private diary in which he may note that age has destroyed your sparkle, that you seem burned out, that you are dull, in short that you bitterly disappointed him. And it is upon this that future biographers, not realizing that anger alone caused your silence, will base their view that you were a miserable old devil.

Do not hope to appease the chronophage by giving him a lump of your time to chew over. His appetite is insatiable. As a dog to whom a guest has foolishly given a piece of chicken comes back to the hand that fed him and keeps on begging with eye and paw until more blackmail has been paid, so the chronophage takes ferocious advantage of any kind and foolish heart he may chance to find. Your forbearance only encourages him to write and pester you again and again.

"I've a lot to do," you say shyly.

"Really," says the chronophage. "How interesting! What are you working on now?"

"A novel!"

"A novel? But my whole life is a novel."

That sets him off. At midnight he will still be there. If he can drag you to his home, you are lost. You are the bone he has dragged to his basket, and he will gnaw you to the marrow. And if he introduces you to his friends, a whole army of chronophages devour you. They are social insects and only too pleased to share their prey.

The moral of this is that the chronophage needs rough treatment; in fact he should be destroyed without mercy. Kindness and restraint are ineffective. On the contrary they create the climate in which the chronophage flourishes. He is a healthy brute: he must be stamped out. I loathe brutality, but in this case it is a duty. You will not let a wild animal tear you to pieces without putting up some resistance, yet the chronophage takes your life as much as a wild animal, for what is your life but time? "Where is the man who sets some value on his time, who knows the worth of a day and who realizes he is dying every instant? While we put things off until tomorrow, life slips away. Nothing is ours, Lucilius, save only our time. And yet we let the first comer deprive us of our sole and fleeting fortune."

That, my dear, was what Seneca wrote to his friend Lucilius two thousand years ago, and it only goes to show that the chronophage is as old as society. But above all do not, having come upon me in a moment of bad temper, go away and deprive me of your company or count every second we are together. A pretty woman can never become a chronophage and she fills our time most preciously. *Adieu.*

Toujours La Politesse?

My dear, be on your guard against politeness for it is a quality which makes men and women commit more follies than their worst faults.

Two fables I'll tell to show the truth of this—of which are many proofs.

The closest friend of a middle-class couple in Paris was the surgeon Professor B, a worthy man, an honor to his profession and a master of his art. But we all grow old and the day came when the lancet trembled in a hand no longer as steady as it had been. His colleagues spread the news and soon all Paris heard that B had had his accidents. Now it came about just then that the husband of this family, so closely connected with the B's, fell ill. His doctor examined him and treated him and finally told him that an operation was essential.

"Who is your surgeon?" he asked.

The patient named Professor B. The doctor made a face.

"He was a master in his day, he is still a good consultant but . . ."

The couple put their heads together. Could they offend poor B by calling in one of his colleagues? They were both quite definite in deciding this would be too cruel.

"How rude," said the wife, "And to think that it was only last week they asked us to dinner."

This argument was unanswerable and decisive. B was called in; only too glad to be of service, he accepted.

"In any case," he said. "It will be the hand of a friend."

Indeed it was the hand of a friend, but the patient died. Politely.

And here is my second fable. A young man was often invited by friends of the family to their estate in Normandy. The daughter of the house showed an obvious liking for him, and he knew that her parents hoped that they would marry. But while very fond of her, he did not think her beautiful and had not the slightest desire to be tied to her for the rest of his life.

One evening in the spring, when the weather was mild, the stars were out and the apple trees in blossom, he was rash enough after dinner to express the wish to take a moonlight stroll.

"What a lovely idea," said his hostess. "Marie-Jeanne will go with you."

The two young people went out into the meadow. A pale aura overhung the orchard. You could hardly see the dewy grass. Quite accidentally the girl caught her foot in a hole and fell. Instinctively and naturally the young man caught her. She found herself in his arms. Their lips were close.

"Ah," she said throbbingly, "I always knew you loved me."

To undeceive her needed ruthlessness and presence of mind, neither of which the young man possessed. He accepted the inevitable. Their lips closed in the fatal kiss. When they went in, they were engaged. He spent all his life with this woman who, in the words of Swann, "was not his sort."

Querida, whenever you think it necessary, be savagely rude. *Adieu.*

Are You Subject or Object?

A woman, as well you know, can be "subject" or "object." She is a "subject" when she remains a personality independent of the man she loves, having her own ideas, making her own plans, mistress of her body and her mind. She is an "object" if she allows herself to be treated as something beautiful and precious perhaps, yet lacking volition, submitting to the desires and caprices of her master, as a delicious morsel which he tastes when he is hungry.

For centuries woman was an 'object." In wars of antiquity she was part of the spoils. The conquering hero took gold and silver cases and slaves as his right of arms. Everything was on the same footing. It was not so very long ago that Paris had her slave market where women could be bought as fruit and vegetables are bought at Les Halles today. Woman had first to gain her economic independence before she could become a "subject" and successfully defend her freedom.

You may remark that many men regret the passing of the "object-woman." How handy she was! She gave pleasure, produced children and then brought them up; she kept house. And in exchange all she asked were food, lodging, et cetera. And did she even demand the et ceteras? After a short enough interval the husband took his attentions elsewhere; her lover would simply desert her.

In those days the woman who claimed to be a "subject" annoyed the men. This was the entire misfortune of George Sand. She was a human being and she asked to be treated as such. Being more intelligent than the majority of men, she maintained her opinions against theirs. She had her own ideas. Like a man, she broke off an affair when she became tired of it. She earned her own living and claimed the right to administer her own fortune. Her poor husband, overwhelmed and routed, complained, "I didn't marry a woman. I married a man."

And this was the reproach that all her generation leveled against Madame Sand; she was too much of a man. Yet on the contrary she was very feminine, physically, in manner, in feeling and even intellectually. But she was a "subject-woman," not an "object-woman": that was the snag.

The other day I lectured in a large town in France on this very theme and I said that, for my part, I accepted the "subject-woman." I admitted that as a young man I should have been very glad to be surrounded by beautiful "object-women," as I would have to own pedigreed dogs, and I admitted that this feeling was nothing more than a barbarous survival. In short I wound up by saying that I respected the human personality in my sisters, the women, as much as I did in my brothers, the men.

A delightful dinner followed at which some very pretty women discussed their own status with their husbands. Many complained that they were still treated, in our own day, as objects. However, one of them plumed herself on this very fact.

"I love to be a luxury object," she said.

"You?" cried her husband. "Why you're the most imperious subject I've ever met!"

And you, *Querida*? Are you subject or object? Tell me? *Adieu*.

Career Woman

There was a time, and not so long ago, when most women neither knew, nor wished to know any other sort of work than that of keeping the house clean and tidy, and bringing up their children. Others did follow a career, often in conditions of hardship and injustice (women then received less pay for the same

113

work as men). Even for those who wished only to be housewives and mothers the husband's job raised problems. Theirs was the task on the one hand of encouraging and supporting him, while not embarrassing him with their inadequacy.

In married life today the question of the career has become one of prime importance because most women have a job. The cost of living is high; unearned incomes have gone down in value while expenditures have risen. For a family to enjoy a full life, two incomes or two wage packets are not too many. This new state of affairs raises new problems. Is it desirable for a husband and wife to follow the same career? If so, should they follow it together? If not how can their differing ways of life be reconciled?

Let us take the oldest, and nowadays the least common, situation in which the husband alone has a career. How can his wife help him? In the first place it is hard to draw a line in a vast majority of cases between home and business. On the land the wife plays an essential part in running and working the farm. In the small shop the wife will serve behind the counter, arrange the goods in the window, and keep the books. If the shop, café or hotel opens out from the living quarters, it is only natural for the owner's wife to run backwards and forwards between her children and her husband's customers. When he is away she is the one to take charge, and she is often the better of the two.

Even when the husband's home and place of business are distinct, the wife can have an enormous influence. If she is clever and tactful, she can make a powerful contribution toward the good relations between her husband and his seniors and colleagues. By taking all the household burdens from his shoulders, she allows him to save all his energies for forwarding his career. But on the other hand if she is peevish and indiscreet she can ruin her husband's best chances of success. A sweet-tempered woman is her husband's refuge in misfortune. A shrew is "like a leaky roof": she annoys without sheltering.

One important point, especially in France, is that a woman should never, except in moments of real danger, act as a brake on her husband. By comparison with other people, the Frenchman does not cultivate enough the taste for taking risks, and if he embarks on a difficult project but which still offers a reasonable chance of success, his wife will best serve her own and her country's interests by supporting him and even by preaching boldness and perseverance. She will do this more effectively and she will carry more conviction, if she has a knowledge of business. Nowadays girls are given a scientific education. They need it, both to understand the ever-increasing hoard of gadgets that simplify their housework and too so as to take an interest in the career of a husband who may be a nuclear physicist, brain surgeon or engineer in an atomic energy establishment. The understanding of the wife will draw the couple together.

Is it desirable for her to follow the same profession as her husband? As I have just said, it is practically essential in the case of farms, small businesses and hotels, but there are other and more complicated professions. Would the husband who is a writer, doctor, civil servant, engineer, film director, or journalist want his wife to be in the same office or even the same line of business? I do not think so. Of course you can imagine husband and wife tracing parallel courses in the same career. If they are both high-minded enough, their rivalry can remain perfectly compatible with their love for each other. But if either of them has the slightest suspicion of envy and vanity, or is even easily discouraged, a similar career can raise serious difficulties.

Particularly if the wife is more talented or more successful than her husband: in spite of himself he will often feel jealous. It is ridiculously unfair, but men have been used to playing the dominant role in marriage for so long that they have a feeling of outraged dignity when they find themselves beaten on their own ground. I knew a theater couple whose marriage was based on mutual love and who seemed at first to be perfectly happy together. Gradually the wife showed that she was an actress of genius. Producers and dramatists entrusted her with increasingly important parts. But her husband was a second-rate actor who never managed to score a hit. He was very unhappy. His wife tried to nurse his injured pride but facts unfortunately spoke all too clearly. In the end, their marriage broke down. Men are like that, my dear. *Adieu.*

Career Woman SECOND LETTER

You can think of solutions to the problems we have discussed. Our first is for the wife to work *with* her husband and help to buttress his self-confidence and to guide him in his decisions. A woman who has been a nurse or a doctor and who marries a doctor can, by accepting a supporting but essential role, insure that their marriage is built on firm foundations. The same thing applies to the woman who has learned typing and shorthand, and who becomes the secretary to a husband who is a journalist, script writer, or author. Nothing rivets a couple so strongly as a common interest in work. They are working partners as well as marriage partners. They are never at a loss for something to talk about, and because their interests are united there can be no question of disruptive influences. Their marriage is even more complete and strong from this very fact.

This division of duties often demands considerable self-sacrifice from the wife. I once met a couple: they were both doctors: as students they had both shown remarkable promise, and both had been internes, and the wife could have had as successful a career as her husband. Yet she took it upon herself to be no more than his assistant. The important discoveries, which were in fact the fruits of their joint research, were all published in her husband's name. One day, when I was praising her self-effacement, she replied: "Don't give me undue credit, I feel no bitterness. Far from it. When a couple are really united there is no such thing as the husband's discoveries or the wife's. They are one and indivisible. My husband's fame is my own, and reflects on me." Her own life proved the truth of her assertions, for the years only drew them closer together.

Very different questions are raised when husband and wife each follow different professions. If the wife triumphs as a high executive, film star or politician while the husband is only moderately successful, or fails completely, she too will need infinite tact and good sense to make him accept a situation, which in the present climate of ideas men still think unnatural. A happy solution is to link the life of the husband to that of his startlingly successful wife in a way which still preserves his self-respect. He can become the guiding force behind his wife's genius. Is she a dress designer whose creations are quite fabulous: then let him become her company secretary. Is she the film star who is the rage of four continents; then let him be her manager. A little modesty, lavish praise, and real love, and the marriage will be saved.

When a married woman works with other men, or under a chief who is a man, the problem of jealousy arises. There is a risk that intimacy, or at all events friendly relations will be established between a man and a woman who see each other every day and who share the common interest of their work. As a result a woman can feel she is much closer to those whose daily anxieties she shares and who help her to master her job, than she does to a husband whom she only sees at the end of a hard day. In these circumstances a woman must be very careful in her relations with her chief and her colleagues and perfectly open in her dealings with her husband if their marriage is to be kept off the rocks. In cases where two professions conflict there lies a very real danger. Holiday time for one is inconvenient to the other, or else one of them is forced to travel, for business reasons, while the other from necessity or choice would like their home life to be calm and undisturbed. But these are conflicts that suit our age when the tensions in the business world grow less only to increase in the emotional sphere. A woman must try to strike the balance between business and private life.

In this modern age a girl's lot is much happier. Her job is the source only of benefits. Not only does she earn her own living, but her life becomes richer and more interesting than it was in the restricted circle of her family. In Balzac's day a girl had to marry the man her parents chose for her because she knew no one else. Today, thanks to her job, a girl meets plenty of young men, and through working with them she is enabled to judge them. In the old days the fiancé whom she would only have met on formal visits, revealed nothing of himself. The daily life of the factory, laboratory or hospital shows up his virtues or his vices unforgettably. Furthermore a girl who knows she can look after herself marries because she wants to, not because she has to; her job at once is her protector and her guide.

All things considered, I think that she will give herself the greatest chance of happiness if she chooses a man whose career she is able and willing to share. Nothing in the world is more delightful than a marriage in which everything, mind and body, success and failure, in short the intimacies of marriage and problems of business are shared. *Adieu.*

Sweet Recollection

Sweet recollection ... is the name of a book by Guillaume Apollinaire which you should read. Nowadays love letters are so few and so short and these will fascinate you. And then they suit you so exactly, they too were written to an unknown woman.

It was the first of January, 1915. At Nice, Bombardier Kostrowitzky (know to literature as Guillaume Apollinaire, his first two names) had boarded the train for Marseilles and found himself alone in his compartment with a charming girl, Madeleine P— He loved poetry, and flirtation and began to flirt and recite Baudelaire, Verlaine, Villon ... Apollinaire, and the unknown knew the same poems by heart. "And yet," she wrote, "he spoke, or rather murmured them so simply that I could never match him: amazed, overwhelmed I surrendered to his voice the poems I myself had begun." Nicely put.

He was leaving for the front, she for Algeria. They exchanged addresses and soon an almost daily flow of letters began to pass between them. As he wrote, seated on a sack of fodder, the paper supported on a tree trunk, the bombardier pictured to himself the eloquent little traveler, with her long eyelashes. He was a poet and a cavalry man and the letters he enjoyed composing, are a delight to read, studded with couplets and quatrains:

It is the gallop of memory among the lilacs of bright eyes
And the guns of indolence fire my dreams toward the skies.

Do you find it strange, *Querida*, that he should have poured out such a flood of love in writing to an unknown girl whom he met for three hours and had not even kissed? I find it the most natural thing in the world. Stendhal and Proust have made it a commonplace that the lover should feel more deeply than the object of his love. An unknown woman crosses his path, his love overflows and he "crystallizes" upon her. Women have been best loved when least seen by their lovers. Dante knew nothing of Beatrice, Stendhal's most passionate affairs took place in his imagination, the "beautiful girl" of *Remembrance of Things Past* was half glimpsed on a station platform. In fact Apollinaire's letters, which burned so strongly at a distance, as to reflect an unbridled passion, only cooled off after he had been on leave and seen his beloved again. "Woman's strongest weapon is her absence." See how strong you are, my dear.

If the poetry hidden in this book gives you a taste for his writing and you go on to read Apollinaire's other love letters, you will discover that he often wrote to three different women on the same day and, at times, used, with minor alterations, the same poem for all three. Does that shock you? But you are wrong, my dear. Every lover who ever put pen to paper has done the same. Chateaubriand was quite capable of sending Madame de Castellane a copy of the letter he had originally written to Madame Récamier. And poems above all! Why abstain from using so fine a weapon or use it only once? But, say you, this lack of sincerity appalls you? *Querida*, poets *are* sincere. The three women to whom an Apollinaire or a Chateaubriand writes, are one woman, a Sylph of his imagination. He needs to give her this series of human forms. Unless he does, he cannot produce poetry. As Byron wrote:

> *Think you, if Laura had been Petrarch's wife*
> *He would have written sonnets all his life?*

So remain my Unknown. *Adieu.*

Take Him As You Find Him

"The male character," she said, "is so different from the female that an inexperienced woman thinks even the most straightforward of men a monster from another planet. To every woman, the man she loves presents a difficult problem. A really shrewd, or even a normally sensible woman tries to find the solution by taking the available facts into account. She says to herself: 'He is thus and thus; how strange; but since I love him as he is, how can I adapt myself to him?' The demanding and passionate woman will not accept the facts of the case, which are the physical and mental traits of her husband or lover: in her innocence she thinks she can reshape him.

"Instead of thinking: Given his nature, how can I make him happy? the Masterful Woman muses: How can I change his nature so that he will make me happy? Because she loves him, she wants him completely to resemble the ideal of the perfect man she draws from her daydreams and books. She persecutes, criticizes, and nags him. And she blames him for saying and doing things which she would laughingly accept from another man.

"Her answer would be that her attitude only proves the strength of her feelings: that in fact if she asks less from others, it is more from indifference than tolerance, and that it is only natural for her, having given her heart to one man and one man only, to try at least to see in him a man who is to her taste; in short that if she reads him lectures they are only for his own good, and that he has made great progress since she took him in hand. . . . This is all very true, but men, unfortunately, have not the slightest desire to 'make great progress' and character cannot be molded like putty.

"A man, a youth, even, is the product of all his ancestors, of the family into which he was born, of his education, and of all that he has experienced. Physically he is what he is: his habits are fixed; his tastes formed. Perhaps it is still possible to correct some of his failings, but only very gradually and only by being very, very careful and taking every precaution your love can suggest, moistening him with compliments as a sculptor moistens the clay when it hardens under his fingers. Direct and violent criticisms will only set a man on the defensive. Love which should be a refuge and a support will bristle with a menacing array of rules and regulations. If he is deeply in love, he will at first put up with them; he will try to improve, then, falling back into his true ways, he will heap curses on the head of her who thwarts him; his love will wither and die and perhaps he will come to loathe wholeheartedly the woman who tried to steal his most treasured possession—his self-confidence. In this way women who are too sensitive create the hidden tensions of married life."

Here I interrupted.

"Aren't you being a little hard on your own sex?" I asked her. "You have only mentioned the mistakes the woman can make. Don't you think that the man, even more than the woman, should accept the facts and recognize that the woman he loves has a character

123

which he should respect and not attempt to change?"

"My dear," she said, "if there still are women who are silly enough to ask a man not to be selfish, clumsy and dogmatic, we must consider them as hopeless cases."

Adieu.

Take Him As You Find Him SECOND LETTER

"It is a small thing to *accept* people for what they are: if we really love them we must *want* them to be what they are." When the philosopher Alain made this remark he taught us something great and noble. We all know plenty of women whose resignation is pained. They accept their husband and children "for what they are," but that does not prevent their complaining. "I didn't have a decent chance," they say, "I could have married a much more capable and brilliant husband, who would have made a far greater success of his life. I could have had far more affectionate and intelligent children. I know I can't change them. I take what Fate has given me, but when I see one of my friends whose husband is quite outstanding and whose children have passed their exams with honors, I have moments of envy and regret. It's only natural."

"No, Madame, it is not natural." Or at all events it is not if you love your family. When you really love a person, you love his faults as well. Without them he would not be himself, and he would not have the characteristics that bind you to him. Your children are behind the others at school? Perhaps, but aren't they more cheerful and natural? Your husband lacks authority? But isn't he kinder? The same thing applies to the character as it does to the body. When you love a person very much, you no longer notice how cranky or how wrinkled he may be. I know that a lady of whom I am very fond, has no great knowledge of the arts and that if she discusses them she is sure to make some appalling mistake. What does it matter to me? She does not make me blush: I know she has a thousand other virtues. A person is a whole person and cannot be changed. He would no longer be my husband: my children would no longer be themselves.

Real love makes all the difference. Does your husband use the same expressions all too often? Others may laugh at him, but you have got used to his ways and you like them. Has he got pet political foibles? They make you laugh and you come to share them. "But," you will say, "what will happen if his failings kill my love for him?" In that case you either only love him moderately or you want patience. It takes a little while to get used to living with someone, even with your children when they grow up. What I am trying to say is that a person can be regarded in two lights. In the first you watch him with a severely, if justly critical eye—the attitude of indifference. In the second with good-humored kindness: you see his failings just as plainly but you laugh at them and only make the gentlest and lightest attempts to correct them. That is the attitude of affection.

And how can you prove that you would have been happier if other people had been different? Would a more ambitious husband have necessarily made you lead

125

a more pleasant life? Who can tell? High office brings in its train grave anxiety and heavy responsibility. The risk of losing it is always there and the disappointment is correspondingly greater. Even if you keep it, what real pleasure does it bring? Hardly has an honor been gained than you have forgotten it and aim for the next. In short you can only eat what your stomach will hold. Affection blooms better in modest circumstances than in the deserts of power. Your sole misfortune is to believe yourself unfortunate, and to feast your imagination on what you have not got instead of enjoying what you have. Say to yourself: "My husband may be shy, but it only makes him kinder to me. My children may not be geniuses but they are loving and good."

Then you will be happy. For happiness is no more than not having the slightest desire to change those whom we love. I accept you as unknown and unknow-able. *Adieu.*

Vitamin A.D.

Querida, you know as well as everyone that the great Victor Hugo, until recently of such re-pute, was for fifty years worshiped like a god by Juliette Drouet: you know how she wrote more than twenty thousand letters to him in which she expressed the same things in twenty thousand different ways, (she had a real genius for ringing the changes) "You are the greatest, the most handsome. . . . My beloved, forgive me for loving you too much. . . . To see you is to live, to hear you, to think, to kiss you is heaven. . . . Good morning you whom I love, good morning. How are you today? I can only bless you, worship you, and love you with all my soul."

And I hear your retort, you cruel sneering Amazon.

"Fifty years of adulation? God! How she must have bored him!" But you are wrong, my dear, you mustn't think that. I know that I myself have often told you of that needful touch of fickleness. I know that there are plenty of men and women who, to the end, despise the one who surrenders, and who pursue the one who rejects them. I know how often Hugo was unfaithful to poor Juliette, even when she was still very lovely, and that she suffered terribly as a result of it. But the others passed like a ripple on the stream and she lasted, all his life.

She lasted because there is a certain type of man, the type who must struggle, the type for whom self-confidence is a vital weapon, the artist, the politician or the great man of action, and this type needs his daily dose of faithful admiration. Adoration, admiration, even adulation, these are all products of the same family and they contain Vitamins A and D. If such a man lacks them his whole strength of purpose is weakened. The body needs calcium and phosphorous; the spirit, encouragement and respect. The body blossoms out in the sunlight, the spirit in the sunshine of love.

Monotony? I agree that undoubtedly she wearied him at times. I am all too sure that Victor Hugo did not read every one of Juliette's twenty thousand letters. You can imagine the triumphant mornings when, on the full tide of inspiration, and eager to return to his desk, he would open his mistress' poor little note, see at a glance that it was the usual mixture, run his eye down to the closing formula: *"Alas I love you more than ever, that is as I did on our first night,"* and would negligently consign the daily letter to its special box. And even the times when, in love with another woman, he searched his mail for letters in a hand not Juliette's, while hers he did not even bother to open.

But come moments of danger, disgrace or disgust, intrigues against the author or persecutions of the man, then while the ambitious lion-hunting hostess pursued other game, the unchangeable Juliette found herself, in ostracism or in exile, alone again with her poet. It was then that the daily note with its tender formula helped the great beast, wounded and hunted, to recover his strength: it was then that Victor Hugo wrote the poems for his Juliette in which, after all these years, he tried to define what their love had come to mean.

> *From the two hearts which it once took is made one heart. From the memory of a common past it has made it impossible for the one to live without the other (Is it not so, Juliette? This is our life!) It has the calm of evening and the noonday glare. It has become friendship while still remaining love!*

Don't you think that it was well worth a prodigality of adoration in youth to receive such verses as an old woman? Come, my dear, write a tender letter to me at once, full of admiration and I promise you a sonnet for your silver wedding. *Adieu.*

Do you like pastiches, my dear? I always think that they are a clever form of criticism. Well I had the chance of writing one this week. The candidates for the *baccalauréat* had been set this question. "Portray a modern businessman in the style of La Bruyère." A newspaper asked some writers to attempt it. This was my answer.

A CHARACTER

Peiratès lives only for his business; stuffed with riches his ventures encompass the globe. "Peiratès, you hold all the sugar refineries in the kingdom, surely that is enough?"—"Do you dream?" said he. "How can I bear the thought of another enriching himself by supplying me with cane? I must have a plantation in the Indies."—"You have it, Peiratès, are you satisfied?"—"And these cotton fields?" he asked.—"You have just bought them; will you stop now?"—"Why?" he said. "Should I not build looms to use up all this cotton?"—"It is done: surely now is the time for repose?"—"Wait," said Peiratès, "a financier draws his interest from this. He offends me." "Turn banker."—"One factory sells me trucks and another machinery. I rage."—"Turn manufacturer."—"My trucks use oil."—"Sink wells, Peiratès. Now you own a chain of factories and plantations that are most marvelously interdependent. You need now rely on no man. Will you at last enjoy life?"

He has no thought of it. Peiriatès has neither desire, nor joy. Rising with dawn each morning he applies himself to his orderly account books and sees the increase of his ever swelling millions, but happiness is for others. What are your pleasures, Peiratès? Sacrificed to the press of business, your wife has long been no more than a frightened crone enmeshed in pearls. Your children are careless of the cares you bequeath them. The money lenders spread their nets for them and their follies would be your despair, if your indifference did not surpass your rage. You have no evening to caress the mistress that costs you so dearly. How can you draw friendship to you, who can only bear flattering parasites?

Rest? Leisure? Peiratès, you refuse what the poorest demand. *Non otium sed negotium* is not an epigram but a rule of conduct in your eyes. Each room of your country house has its telephone, and there is even one beside the pool in which your doctor commands you to plunge your wasted frame from time to time. You have so much money that you are ever anxious for its value on the Stock Exchange. Once books and music pleased you, but you have long lost the taste for them. You keep the prince of cooks, and yet you regret the cabbage soup that bubbled on your poor mother's cottage fire. Continue your delightful task, Peiratès. Dig ports, own fleets of aircraft, build radio stations and atomic piles, the advances of science bring you, you lucky man, fresh opportunities of killing yourself in useless toil. If perchance your affairs are insufficient, those of the state may demand your care. You know yourself capable of command, and you have often said that all would go better if the country were governed in the same fashion as your businesses. Are we to understand, Peiratès, that it should be ruled in such sort as to increase your wealth still more?

Meanwhile, Peiratès grows old, and I see him, for the first time almost content. It is because he has had a stroke of genius. To spare the children he hates the costs of inheritance, he has bought a law firm in the name of one of his clerks, who has promised to restore the fees to the family. This is our hero's happiest venture which one must rejoice that he had time to conclude for he died setting his seal to it. This morning I learned of his death.

But was Peiratès ever a man? He was a businessman. That is different.

A professor corrected my composition; he did not know its author's name and he gave me eighteen, *querida*, and my pride is boundless. *Adieu.*

The Constant Nymph

American sociologists adore statistics and have profound faith in polls. This is doubtless due to the fact that in their own country they take such things seriously. Everyone makes an effort to answer their questions truthfully. And so it is hard for them to realize that most Frenchmen, however strongly their anonymity may be guarded, dislike baring their inmost souls, so that the answers such polls produce here are noncommittal or downright false.

One of these young American public opinion tasters, came to see me yesterday, brimful of enthusiasm, and told me:

"I am writing a thesis on the influence of women in French life. In your books you often mention the importance of the salon in your national history. I've read authorities on Madame du Deffand, Madame Récamier, Madame de Loynes, and Madame Arman de Caillavet. Do you think that you have today women powerful enough to influence, for example, an election to the Académie Française or to push a man to President du Conseil?"

"You have," I answered, "raised two very different questions, of very different importance. No! No one woman in our day can influence an election to the Académie Française. In the first place no one I know has friends in all the diverse groups that make up the Academy. And then there are quite a number of independents at the *quai Conti*, men with a taste for solitude, who never set foot in a salon, who do not dine out, and who are, in fact, inaccessible. How could a woman influence their vote?"

"You have no Madame Récamier, then, today?"

"Madame Récamier had at her command one vote, perhaps two or three, though I very much doubt it. Of course a woman can get a promise of a vote but the vote itself is a very different thing. And when it comes to making a President du Conseil, she needs to obtain three hundred and twelve; how the devil do you suggest she goes about it? The most she can do, if she is clever, is to be a catalyst, bringing together the heads of warring parties and dispersing their misunderstandings. But her task will be one of preparation rather than actual execution. She will create the favorable set of circumstances; what ensues no longer depends on her.

"And yet," said he, "in France you still talk about your Egerias."

"Egeria," I replied, "was the nymph who inspired Numa Pompilius. He claimed that he met her in a sacred grove and that she advised his politics. A sensible way of winning the confidence of a superstitious people, but Egeria was never more than a myth. She still is: mind you, while I do not believe a woman can secure power for a man, I will admit that she plays a leading part in making him fit for it. In France many of our future statesmen are still very provincial when they first begin their careers. They have intelligence and eloquence; but they have neither the niceties of manner nor of conversation, which they need if they are to conquer Paris. Such a man can have no better luck than to be taken under the wing of a woman who, partly from love, partly from ambition, sets herself the task of training him. Be she actress, society woman or merely a woman of culture, she polishes this rough diamond and teaches him the secrets of Paris and who the people are that really count in her various social circles. But this is nothing new. Reread your Balzac and in particular the admirable plan for living, which, in *Lys dans la vallée*, Madame de Mortsauf set her young lover."

"Then you do admit that, in the Balzacian sense, Egeria still exists?"

"And will exist too for as long as there are men and women and governments."

Wasn't I right, *Querida?* You better than anyone should know. *Adieu.*

First Love

His first love affair marks a man for life. If it brings him happiness and if the woman or girl who first awakes his youthful passion reciprocates it and keeps faith with him, the man's whole existence will be wrapped in an atmosphere of calm confidence. But if, when for the first time he is prepared to place his entire trust and being in one person's hands, she ignores him or betrays him, the wound will never completely heal and he will take a long time to recover his mental balance.

Not that such disillusionments produce the same effects in everyone. Love is a disease whose symptoms are vague. Scorned by Mary-Ann Chaworth for his deformity, Byron became a Don Juan and made all women pay for her cruelty. Rejected for his poverty by Maria Beadnell, Dickens became the autocratic husband, ever ready to find fault, never satisfied. But in both cases the first disappointment prevented their ever making a happy marriage.

Frequently the man whose first affair has been unhappy is obsessed for the rest of his life by the woman of his dreams, a compound of poetry and romance, virgin and mother, companion and mistress, imperious and submissive. He is faithless because he chases this will-o-the-wisp. Instead of accepting women as they are, imperfect, hard to understand but nonetheless real, he seeks an angel, as the romantic poets say, and becomes a beast.

134

Sometimes when a young man has been disappointed by women of his own age he turns to the woman of forty. She at least will be loving because her love will be infinitesimally tinged with the maternal instinct, and because, knowing that she will soon be doomed to old age, she will make every effort to keep the young man. Balzac, whose love life began with a mistress older than he, as a result retained a life-long self-confidence, a bouncing ingenuousness, which sustained him in his worst moments. In addition the woman of thirty-five or forty is a much surer guide to the ways of the world than a girl who is quite ignorant of life and its difficulties.

But it is hard to keep the balance later on in a marriage of this sort. For true happiness nothing can match a marriage of two people of about the same age, the husband the elder, in which there are no reservations, and in which both loyally accept the other's love, freely binding themselves to keep faith because they understand each other completely. When first love is the only love, life is wonderful. But it means that girls must give up the joys of flirtation and that is hard. But perhaps the misfortunes of Byron will teach them what dangers lie in the little cruelties that they think so harmless. It is heavy responsibility, my dear, to be the first love of a man who is a genius—and indeed of any man. *Adieu.*

Heavenly Music

How I love the country! Such stillness. Such quiet. The certainty that the long day will not be torn to shreds by callers or telephone bells. This is really to rediscover time. In our cities we squander those precious days which, few as they are, are all we have; we forget that life is but an instant and that we should make that instant, short as it is, as wonderful and as perfect as we can. When I stand before this cedar and these century-old limes, when I see the eternally repeated pattern of the harvest, and when in the evening I look up at the starry sky, then at last the minutes are filled as they should be.

Friends? We have books and records and they complement each other marvelously. Yesterday, I had been asked to write a preface, and I was reading Tolstoy's *Kreutzer Sonata*. It is a searing and terrible novel, torn out of the author by the battle within himself between his satyr's temperament, which craved incessantly for women, and his rigid moral code, which commanded his absolute chastity. As marginal comment are the words of St. Matthew: "I say unto you whosoever shall look lustingly upon a woman has already committed adultery with her in his heart." Yes, says Tolstoy, even if that woman is his own wife: "the worst form of depravity is between husband and wife." We conceal, he adds, the animal aspect of physical love under a cloud of poetic nonsense. We are pigs, not poets, and it does us good to be reminded of that fact. He particularly attacks the erotic influence of music.

"Music," says the hero of the book, "is sexually exciting but that is not its true purpose. When Beethoven wrote the *Kreutzer Sonata*, he was well aware why he was in a certain state of mind: this state of mind led to certain actions, logically for him, but for no one else! It is fearful to think of this power being placed in the hands of any and everyone. . . . What right have they to play this *Kreutzer Sonata* in a room full of half naked women. . . . To generate an emotional energy unsuited to time and place can only have dangerous results." What obsesses the archetype of the husband, who uses these words, is the thought that sooner or later his wife will fall into the hands of the violinist who stirs her senses in this way. This is in fact what does happen, and the husband with the savagery of a wild beast, kills his wife.

What a marvelous book, I thought as I closed it. Less a novel than a cry. Poetry that rages like the *Colère de Samson?* but is it true? Is music to blame? I am passionately fond of Beethoven (in spite of all those who follow the present fashion of blaming him for being repetitious) but I have never found his music sensual. Tender, if you like, soothing, comforting; sometimes sublimely strong as in the *Hymn to Joy*, at others sympathetic and friendly as in the Andante to the *Symphony in C Minor* . . .

In our house in the country we have the recording of the *Kreutzer Sonata* made by Yehudi Menuhin and his sister. "We shall see!" I said to myself, and we gave ourselves a Beethoven evening.

Tolstoy was wrong. There was nothing lascivious or baleful about this music. It was heavenly and sublime. At

137

times it made me think of the more than human choirs of angels that dominate Fauré's *Requiem*. Night fell. In the dark we listened to the duet of brother and sister, pure sounds. It was a heavenly evening. This is the sort of thing the country alone can give. *Adieu*.

Taking the Plunge

The countryside is steeped in vast silence. The fields scorched by the sun and the village at the head of the valley sleeps in the mist. This morning I started a book. You will tell me that this is not of the slightest concern to you and that I am wrong in thinking that this trifling event merits such an announcement, *urbi et orbi*. I agree that it is not of world-shaking importance and I only mention it for the useful lesson it can teach you, me and all of us.

Writing is not easy, but choice of subject is the hardest thing in the world. A novelist or biographer is offered an almost limitless number of themes from which to choose. A *Life of George Sand*? Tempting, only there are ten other studies of the subject. A little known hero? An American publisher wrote to me: "There are relatively few Lives that appeal to the public here: Christ, Napoleon, Lincoln, Marie Antoinette, and two or three others." No doubt something new can be written about any subject by using either new documents or an original approach. But if it is a theme which has tempted hundreds of researchers before you, you will be buried under piles of articles and books. On the other hand if your subject is unexploited you will be drowned in an ocean of indecipherable and unpublished documents.

In short every book seems to its author impossible to write. And this is just as true for the novelist as it is for the biographer. "That story? Yes, but it is far too auto-biographical. . . . That one? But my friends would be furious to find themselves in it. That one? Far too thin. . . . That one? Over elaborate." There is only one remedy for this: *Begin*. Alain said, "Will without action is an impossibility. Man swims in the universe from the moment he is plunged into it and he is being forever plunged." The rudder is ineffective until the ship is in motion. You cannot learn to write without writing. In this trade, as in any other, shiver in thought for a moment and then take the plunge. Otherwise you can spend a lifetime making up your mind. I have known more than one man of potential talent stand on the brink until Death found him, asking himself, "Have I the strength?"

You have always the strength if you continuously exercise your will power. For the second factor is per-severance. You must swear to finish what you have be-gun. To write a thousand-page book seems a terrifying enterprise. Yet three pages a day for a whole year will do it. I have chosen to write a *Life of Victor Hugo*, and I have promised myself that I will read every word he wrote and every word written on him. It will be a long job but I shall do it. My only mistake would be to stop in the middle and say to myself: "No, it's too hard! I'm going to find an easier subject." The mountaineer hack-ing steps in the snow of a mountain wall cannot go back. His safety is in his courage. That is true of any activity; it is particularly true of writing.

"But," you will tell me, "I haven't the slightest desire to write."

Perhaps: but you want to succeed in other things: sport, gardening, painting, dressmaking. How can I tell? The recipe is always the same. Begin, however clumsy you may feel you are, and persevere. You will be surprised to find experience coming to you as if by magic. Six months ago you could hardly drive along a main road, but now you slip through the thickest traffic in Paris. I come back again to that great man Alain: "Laziness is nothing more than endless deliberation, for in reflection all possibilities are of the same value. . . . One must therefore be able to deceive oneself, into making one's choice, and not go back on it."

I shall not go back on mine, hard though this *Hugo* be. I have chosen and I shall persevere. *Adieu.*

Darby and Joan

There are, my dear, three kinds of enduring marriages. To start with the worst, there is the kind in which the two are tired of each other. Forty years of married life have not drawn them together. They had little in common on their wedding day, and now they have, literally, nothing to say to each other. You can tell them in a restaurant by the silence, never broken by so much as a smile, in which they sit. They ignore each other, only too glad of a respite from their mutual hate. But why do they still live together? Because they are used to it, because they respect conventions, because they conform with their family traditions and because they are unable to find two flats and lead separate lives. Such marriages we deplore.

The second kind is several stages better, consisting of husbands and wives who either have never really loved each other, or no longer do so, but who find in each other a faithful partner. Long years of peaceful coexistence have proved that that partner, while neither lovable nor charming, does have other qualities. He is dependable, honest, and has known over the years how to forgive and accept forgiveness for whatever mistakes may have been made. Couples of this sort are drawn together sometimes by the husband's career, at others by the success they have achieved or by their love for their children or grandchildren. They are insured against loneliness by their family circle and their social contacts.

The third, the admirable sort, consists of long and happy marriages. For the whole art of marriage lies in the ability to pass from love to friendship without sacrificing love. It is not utterly impossible. The white heat of passion sometimes burns to the very end, but where husband and wife are really one, "that magnificent silk, so richly embroidered, is lined with another, simpler, but of so rare and fine a texture that one is tempted to prefer it to what covers it." The dominant note, then, is one of confidence, whose perfection is matched by the degree of mutual understanding which goes with it and an affection so watchful that it foresees the reactions of the beloved.

Boredom cannot get between such people. The husband prefers his wife's company to that of the youngest and prettiest woman; and the corollary is true. Why? Because each knows the other's interests so well and both share so many of the same tastes that they never lack topics of conversation. Their daily walk is as precious now as the lover's meetings which preceded their marriage once were. They know that they not only understand but foresee each other's actions. They think the same thing at the same time. They each suffer physically when the other is upset. To have met a man (or woman) who has never let us down or ever deserted us is something very wonderful.

When a marriage passes unscathed the storms of middle age, it floats into a wonderful calm. There is nothing finer than the serenity of such couples. The thought of death is the only thing which can jar such perfect love. And yet to stake all upon one weak human life is at once the risk that high passion must take and the element that gives it its grandeur. But death itself is powerless against the strongest love. To have something perfect to remember in time of sorrow and loneliness is a real consolation. Furthermore when people have enjoyed a long and happy marriage they live on in the minds of those who have known, loved and admired them.

But what on earth, you will say, is the point of discussing Darby and Joan with a young wife? Because it is sensible to prepare for the future however distant it may be, and, too, because it is the sort of Sunday for sober reflection. A thin misty bluish haze, typically Parisian, cloaks the trees in the Bois below our window, trees that now wear the rich tints of autumnal decay. *Adieu.*

Where Then Is Happiness?

You have written me a harsh and even cruel letter, my dear. "I was rather annoyed," you say, "by your article on optimism. How on earth can any inhabitant of this crazy world be an optimist? Perhaps you do think you are happy but I tell you that in reality you are miserable. Think: you have been thrown haphazard on a globular mass of earth and water revolving in darkness, and that after this planetary carousel has revolved quite pointlessly for a certain number of times, you must die. How can you be calm and contented? You say that your success in life satisfies your modest ambitions? You would like to believe this is so, but you must be only too well aware that your youthful dreams encompassed more brilliant victories. You say that your wife attracts you more than other women and that you have found true happiness in marriage? Come, come. Be frank, isn't this a case of sour grapes? Admit that you sometimes regret the pleasures your marriage vow forbids you. But wait, there is a poem by your beloved Victor Hugo entitled: *Où donc est le bonheur?* (Where then is happiness?) In which he shows that your boasted happiness is no more than a series of misfortunes.

So, my God, man marches in gathering gloom from the cradle's glow to the shadows of the tomb . . . Alas! He is born for a life that longs for death, he grows up regretting the heart's ease of childhood, he ages regret-

143

ting the youth that was snatched from him and dies
regretting that old age and life itself. Where then is
happiness? I said—Wretch! Oh God happiness is what
you have given me.

"Yes, you are given this happiness, and it is no more
than a huge cheat, a lie which lasts our short and futile
life on earth."

You are gloomy today, *querida*: you must have been
reading some dreadful books lately. Do you reproach
me for self-deception, for shutting my eyes to what,
according to you, is the wretchedness of our state as
human beings? But to forget its difficulties, to try not
to think too much about them, to emphasize the most
agreeable aspect of our little joys—our first kiss, our first
love, engagements, honeymoons, our pleasure in watch-
ing our children grow up, the serenity of old age—this
is not self-deception, it is a brave attempt to take life
for what it is. I agree that this life cannot be completely
happy, but the greater part of it can be, and it is up to
us to make it so. Happiness does not lie in outward
events, but in the hearts of those that experience them.
To believe as I do, in happiness is to be happy, for happiness is no more than an attitude of mind. "Where then
is happiness?" It lies within our grasp: it is simple and
commonplace. And it cannot be a lie because it is a
condition of the soul.

If I am hot, I am hot, it is a fact, and it is useless for you
to say, "You deceive yourself, you are wrong to be
hot." What do I care? "It is not because I am warm
that I am happy," said Spinoza. "It is because I am happy
that I am warm." If I love my wife and am happy with
her I *am* happy. You may say, "It won't last. Love always
passes, wearies and dissolves. There are women younger

and prettier than your wife." What do I care? I don't desire younger women. What can you say to that? Happiness cannot live as a lie for once you see that your happiness is a lie it ceases to be happiness. Q. E. D. *querida*. Read Alain's *Propos sur le bonheur* and be careful of these overpessimistic novels—and enjoy this lovely summer. *Adieu*.

Bringing Children Up

The holidays are nearly over and so you ask my advice on educating your children. They may be quite small, but I think that from very early on they get a better upbringing at school than they do at home. The loving father or mother understands them too well, forgives their faults and finds excuses for their laziness, and is more inclined to wipe their eyes than smack their bottoms. School, like life itself, is tough and impartial and if the prettiest little mother's darling fails her exams she must try again or leave. Those are the rules and they are sensible. Children should never be given the impression, from overindulgence, that tears and kisses wipe out mistakes, that life is easy, and that the all-powerful family will settle all. Life is a battle and we should train for it from childhood. School friends are better teachers than parents for they are ruthless.

Do not try to turn education into a series of games. Effort alone sharpens the wits. It is necessary that your son should have some difficulty in understanding what he reads, otherwise he will only give his books cursory and intermittent attention. Set him straight on to the classics. Proust's mother made him read the novels of George Sand and Dickens: the result was Marcel Proust. Make him learn good poetry by heart: Corneille, La Fontaine, Hugo. At first a good many words will be beyond him, but soon he will enlarge his vocabulary. The music of the verses will uplift him. Notice that this is a synonym for *bringing up*. To bring up a child is to lift up his mind and character, to lead him to the mountain tops; and for that purpose he must have guides who are used to those high altitudes—of necessity the poets. And how thankful your children will be to you in after years for having stored their minds so richly. I recall what consolation I found in reciting poetry to myself during the dark days of 1940.

Teach your children at least one manual skill. Nobody knows what the world of tomorrow will be like, but there will always be a place for people who can use their hands. Your children will live in a world of machines: they must really understand them. Machines are hard on those who do not love them. Nowadays every boy should be an electrician, a carpenter and radio mechanic, otherwise he will be the slave for life of every practitioner of these trades.

The wonderful thing about young people is that their brains are still so impressionable that they can pick up languages and manual skills with the greatest of ease. One should therefore take every advantage of this all too short opportunity. Later on the same things will be much harder to acquire. I once had an English friend, Miss Harrison, who taught Greek until she was seventy. When she retired she decided to learn Russian. It was a hard struggle, but she succeeded. At her age she found

it difficult, but a child plays at languages, and furthermore, a child learns by ear and so acquires an impeccable
accent, while a grownup learns by eye and so gives the
foreign tongue the same sound as the equivalent letters
have in his own language. Give your sons English and
Spanish, which are the keys to half the world, and in
addition Latin which will unlock the gates of the imagination.

What else can I tell you? Always act in a way which
will make your children respect you enough to look up
to you and not enough to fear you. Do not expect them
to have virtues which you do not practice yourself.
Young people keep their eyes open and come to their
own conclusions. If they admire you as much as I do all
will be well. There, my dear, is my back to school
speech. Frivolity must wait until tomorrow. *Adieu.*

Vacations and Love

Love, by which I mean more than the
satisfaction of a momentary desire, romantic love needs
time. In a wealthy society with time to spare, for example the Court at Versailles or, nearer our own day,
the world within a world depicted by Proust, such
leisure was never wanting and love was possible at any
time. But after two world wars, in a world in which a
man must work twelve hours a day merely to insure a
livelihood for himself and his family, there is no time for
the charmingly protracted overtures to love.

How many married men in Paris or anywhere else

come home after a hard day's work in the right frame of mind to talk love to their wives? How many men still have the leisure of the hero of Bourget or de Maupassant's novels, in which to visit a mistress between five and seven? I picture to myself a ceiling painted in old-fashioned, allegoric style—*Cupid awaits the Vacation.* On it would be seen crowds of men and women, all the slaves of some machine or other, dashing from factory to bank, and pouring into the subway, while at the side Cupid would be leaning disconsolately against his useless bow, fingering a calendar, and sighing, "Oh July! Oh August!"

In the next room you could see *Cupid during the Vacation.* The painting would be full of pairs of lovers, some lying half naked in the sunshine on the beach, others on the grass, others under the trees, and others walking arm in arm up mountain tracks, while dominating this world of blazing passions would stand Cupid, weary, short of arrows, his supplies constantly being replenished by relays of other little Cupids. For really what else can you do on a vacation but make love? What more favorable time for it than when men and women have nothing more pressing to do, when tours and holiday resorts mix people so marvelously and when you can meet anybody?

For eleven months of the year a young man from Bellac has only the girls of Bellac to meet. He has known them all his life, and it is possible that among them he has found the woman of his dreams. In that case all is for the best in the best of Bellacs. But more often than not he has been unlucky; when all of a sudden his vacation puts him in touch with girls from thirty-six thousand French towns and villages, and under circumstances

148

which are peculiarly favorable to romance: all the time in the world for long heart to heart talks, and the sentimental privacy of walks tête-à-tête. Vacations are open season for Don Juan: Donna Anna lies naked on the sand while the Commendatore goes off with his shrimping net or loses his money at the Casino. For the young husband in love with his wife it is at last the moment to really get to know her.

For there can be two kinds of vacations for married couples: those they take together or those they take separately. For the couple who are happily married the first is the most delightful. At last they truly see each other and find the real person who was under the mask of worry and fatigue. Above all they see each other in fresh surroundings which give their love a delicious dash of the exotic. A husband who can give his wife a fortnight at some really good musical or dramatic festival is lucky. He will enjoy the benefit of feelings aroused by Mozart and Musset. But Nature works just as well. Ocean is a wonderful go-between and the peace of the countryside turns marriage into an idyl. "Tumbled in the hay with only the sun as witness," townsfolk rediscover the springtime of the world, and their own.

Vacations on one's own are only advisable for the sake of the children or for one's health. Of course there are plenty of couples whose relations are so excellent and well founded that they can separate without fear of the consequences. When the heart is on vacation it is not necessarily vacant. They love each other too much to yield to a passing affair. Nonetheless one must not forget that temptation will come, and it will be strong. A pretty wife in a seaside town or a spa, left alone to face the wiles of the bachelors or the poaching of other women's husbands, will find resistance far harder there than in her own little home town where her every action is controlled by her family and the sharp tongues of the old ladies behind their lace curtains. Even on vacation the old ladies are still there and their nose for scandal is just as keen (it is the one compensation for their age) but we do not know them. Their whispers do not matter. The restraint of public opinion is weaker, and in any case it is unnatural to be on one's own; boredom is a natural bawd. "The only thing," said Goethe, "that makes one put up with the unbearable boredom of a cure is a pleasant little flirtation." But a flirtation becomes an affair in real earnest if people see each other all day long.

And so separation, which has its own peculiar charm, has its dangers too, though they are relatively unimportant if the marriage was very shaky before the couple parted. But if it was happy, an accident of this sort would be something to be sorry for: in love the first offense does not cost a two-dollar fine, but the couple's happiness. One way of guarding against this is to keep in touch with long and loving letters every day. I am told that letters are not so well written as they used to be, particularly love letters. I doubt this, but if it is the case, I am sorry. A letter allows you to write so many sentimental loving things which you might be too embarrassed to say to the person's face. Exchanging letters allows you to explain without quarreling. "But without making things up," says a young lady who is reading this over my shoulder. Why? You can make it up when you are together again. "The beauty of letters is in the eye of the writer," she goes on. I don't think so. All love letters are beautiful—in the eyes of the men and women who receive them. The style is the man—or the woman—one loves. And, *querida*, paid vacations are not vacations from fidelity. *Adieu*.

Two Different Sorts of Love

One day, when conversation turned on what really matters in life, Victor Hugo remarked that what he really valued was neither fame, fortune nor genius, but loving and being loved. He was right. Nothing is worth having unless it can be shared with those who love us and love us wholeheartedly, and yet the love adds nothing in itself unless we love them ourselves. Not that they need be many in number. I have often thought that you could be happy in the smallest town, even in some oasis in the Sahara, if only you had two or three real friends there; and contrariwise I do not think that a head of state or a leading figure in the arts can know real happiness, unless there is one person beside him with whom he can remove his mask. Hence is the enormously important part that intimate friends, wives or mistresses, have played in the lives of great men. "One feels so alone," a famous man around whom a little court revolved once told me. Love, either of children, wife or friends, breaks the prison of loneliness.

But there are two different sorts of love. The first is selfish, that is attachments formed with an eye to what they may bring us. Some wives love and truly love a husband who gives them at once security, affection and sexual satisfaction, but they love him because they cannot conceive of a life without him. He is indispensable: he takes care of their and their children's happiness: he is the center of their life. But they hardly consider his life; they never ask themselves whether he has other desires or needs, and they think it perfectly natural that his short span should be entirely spent in providing for the happiness of others.

There is no lack of husbands and lovers of the same sort. They, too, love a woman for what she gives them and never try to fathom her state of mind. Children who love their parents almost always love them in this way. To them their father is the person upon whom one can always rely, their mother the one to whom they can always confide knowing she will be on their side. But how many children make any attempt to lighten their parents' anxieties or to help them in difficulty? That is what I call selfish love.

To love a person for his or her sake is to think not of what he or she gives us but what we give them. It is to implicate oneself so closely in their life and to share their feelings so completely that their happiness comes before our own. Do not, however, think this is something rare. Many parents are happier when their children succeed than they would have been at their own success. I have known plenty of married couples who lived for each other. Some friendships have been sublimely selfless. Balzac has portrayed one such in *Cousin Pons* and another in *Le Messe de l'Athée*. True friendship foresees the needs of others rather than demanding its own. That is what I call loving people for their own sake.

The important point is that unselfish love brings more happiness than selfish love. Why? Because man is so made that forgetting himself helps to make him happy.

As long as he thinks only of himself, he lives in a state of worry and discontent. He is preoccupied with his own position: "Have I got all I could out of life? What mistake did I make to land me where I am? What do people think about me? Am I well liked?" But as soon as another person becomes the center of our lives, doubts are resolved. What must we do? We must make those whom we love happier. From that moment life takes on a new meaning and revolves on a central axis. The extraordinary happiness given by a love for God is not, unfortunately, within the reach of all, but love for his creatures brings its own joy and reward. *Adieu.*

Too Late

The other day I saw a very moving film. It was the perfectly simple story of a destitute old couple who suddenly found themselves dependent upon their children. They were no worse than the rest of us and the parents seemed a nice old pair. But everything turned out badly. The older generation became a burden to the younger, and time destroyed the good relationship between them. The parents were tactless and the children impatient. Sons and daughters-in-law soon refused to put up with relations with whom they had the slenderest ties. In the end the mother was put into an institution where she died.

As I left the cinema I thought of the children's remorse. For, let there be no mistake, they would feel it once their parents were dead. While people are alive we treat them with an involuntary mixture of affection and annoyance. We love them, but we see their failings and those failings irritate us and sometimes make our own lives difficult. We give in to our desires, and even when it is clear that to satisfy them will give pain to those who love us, we lull our consciences with the thought, Of course they will be upset, but I can't always be the one who gives way. In any case I can always make amends by being kinder another time.

But we leave Death out of our calculations. Death is inevitable and then nothing will make amends. Then will come the time of our remorse. Death makes us forget the failings of the dead and leaves us with regret for what we could but did not do. The very tricks of phrase and gesture which once seemed fussy or stupid now become touching and sad once we know we can never see them again. We begin to think of things which would have touched or appeased the dead, things which would have cost so little effort on our part. One word, thinks the son in mourning, a short visit, a telephone call or a letter would have brightened the old man's whole day. And yet I deprived him of his simple pleasure solely to spend a few more minutes with my wife who has me all the time. I found time to write to my superiors and my friends, but I found no time to write to my father. And yet I loved him with all my heart. . . .

I feel no surprise when I read that savages and primitive people fear the dead and try to appease them with sacrifices. It is true that the dead return in dreams to torture the living when they made them too miserable. Read the great novel of Anatole France, *Histoire Comique* on this very point, read too Chateaubriand's confession after the death of Madame Duras, whose faithful friendship he had so often rewarded with unfeeling impatience. "From the day I lost such a generous friend . . . I have not ceased, while mourning her, to reproach myself for the unfairness with which I have sometimes treated people who are devoted to me. We should watch our characters most carefully. We should think how not to sadden the lives of those who love us, lives that we would buy back with our heart's blood. When our friends have gone to the grave, how can we make amends for the injuries we have done them? Can our useless remorse, our vain repentance wipe out our unkindness? They would have far rather had a smile from us while they were alive than all our tears now they are dead."

Never deprive the living of the kindness which you offer their ghosts in vain. Remember this, *querida*, and should we meet, do not lay up vain repentance for the future by upsetting the poor old man that I am. *Adieu.*

The Man Who Would Be King

Kipling wrote a remarkable short story called *The Man Who Would Be King*. It is the tale of an Irish adventurer, a fine soldier, brave as a lion who was obsessed with the idea of ruling a practically unknown country which Kipling calls Kafiristan. Remember that in half barbarous parts of the world, this is not so crazy as it sounds and that not so very long ago an English traveler, Brooke, became Rajah of Sarawak.

At first all goes as our hero wished. He astounds, terrifies and brings these mountaineers who have never seen a rifle under his sway by his marksmanship. Once he is master of one village he trains the inhabitants as soldiers and being a good old Irish sergeant he creates an invincible army. His power extends from peak to peak. The natives take him for a god and obey and worship him. Soon his dreams come true and he is king of a vast country.

And so he would have stayed if he had not been tempted by the women of the country. Why, he thinks, should not the king marry? He imparts his wishes to the priests. They shake their heads. "Can a god take one of the daughters of men as his wife?" But the king has made his choice; a pretty girl is to be his wife. After the ceremony he goes to kiss her. Frightened into hysterics, the girl bites him and his blood flows. It is the signal for revolt. "You are no god, you are only a man!" and his subjects hurl him over a steep precipice.

It is an old story, a story as old as humanity itself. Samson and Delilah was the first rough sketch and it is only natural that this myth should be so old and yet so enduring, because it is so profoundly true. The man who wants to rule must give up the simple pleasures. Hard as it may seem, the leader of men must be a chaste ascetic. To be popular, you have only to share the pleasures of the mass of men, but you will seldom be respected.

We have all of us known the sort of young man who is a tin god in his own *départment*, and who fills increasingly important posts because he is a sound businessman and able to conciliate conflicting interests. Having reached Paris as *deputés* such men are tempted by the brilliance of a new way of life. We have plenty of Delilahs only too ready to snap up these Samsons. All too soon the modest young Parliamentarian gets a taste for dining out and leading a gay life. If he has a generous nature he will want to repay hospitality. Soon he spends in a single night what once would have lasted a whole month. As he has power to sell, a rich racketeer offers to buy it from him. Delilah urges him to accept. Tomorrow his subjects will find he was only a man, and a very weak one at that. The precipice is all too close.

My soul's Unknown, you know whom I have in mind. *Adieu.*

The Present Season

The time for present giving is upon us. I admit I greet it joyfully, not so much for what I shall be given (there are few things I really want) but for the thought behind the gift. The gift that has been lovingly selected stands out from all the rest by the study of the recipient's taste, by the originality of the choice and by the care with which it is given that it presupposes. Hence the invariable popularity of symbols and allusions in this time of Christmas presents. If so many perfumes carry names suggestive of the memories and hopes of lovers, it is because in giving them we are able to express wishes that would otherwise have remained unspoken. The same is true of some novels and poems. Thanks to the season a man in love can make his girl read the novel which he would like her to live. Sainte-Beuve went so far as to write a novel which showed his hopes to the reader. A scarf or a handkerchief says in a printed motto what the sender would never dare write himself. And

diamond arrows flash straight to the heart. Guided mis-
siles.

I enjoy giving presents even more than receiving
them. There is nothing I like better than imagining the
pleasure that will glow in the face of someone I love
when they find that a wish they have made long ago
without much hope of realizing it, has suddenly come
true. Hunting through a toy shop is one happiness we
have for as long as we have children young enough for
us to be able to make them happy. Later on, unfortunately, the present that will really thrill is not ours to give,
and so what a good thing it is that women remain children where presents are concerned. How pleasant it is
to play Santa Claus for their benefit! The only difficulty
is to play it well. Most men tend to think that what
pleases them will please their womenfolk. Nothing could
be further from the truth. Because I admire such and
such a philosopher I would be glad to give his complete works to a woman to whom a scrap of fur, a
modest piece of jewelry or even a bunch of flowers
would have more appeal. Presents should be chosen for
the recipient, not for the giver.

Another thing: a present should be a *real* present, that
is to say a complete, definite and unconditional gift.
Some families give presents on loan. "To give and hold
onto is valueless." Some parents may give their little boy
an electric train. Then with the excuse that he is the
better mechanic, the father plays with it while the child
watches him in sulky frustration. Others continue to
watch over the toys they have given away as though
they were precious and fragile works of art to be placed
in a museum, behind a protective rope.

"Don't hit your doll; you'll break it."

"But, Mummy, she's been naughty."

"Don't be silly: it's only a doll . . . and anyway it cost your father a lot of money."

Killing a child's illusions spoils the day.

"*They* give us presents," the children say, "and then *they* won't let us touch them. If they see us really enjoying ourselves, they shut them up in the cupboard."

More than one Christmas day ends in tears. Remember that "too much" is part of the spirit of the feast. Careful penny counting presents are not presents at all. A very humble gift can thrill the person who receives it always provided that the giver's purse is slender too. "A bunch of flowers given with love is the gift of the whole round world." But if you are rich, you should give a little more than might reasonably be expected. Not to give too much is not to give enough.

If giving is an art, so too is receiving, and it is no less hard. You need imagination. If you cannot picture to yourself as you accept a well-chosen present, the hours of thought and patient search which the donor has put into it, you will be unable to thank him properly. Think how your friend has been enjoying your pleasure for days in advance. Think how he listens for your cry of surprise and astonishment. He hopes his present will be discussed "for long beside the hearth." He wants to hear you go over its beauties one by one and he is waiting for you to boast of his generosity and good taste. A present ill received causes many a painful little scene. A wife with little pin money may buy her husband three ties. He opens the box:

"Is this for me?" he asks. "You should have known by now that I never wear such flashy patterns. In the future kindly let me choose my own things."

159

Floods of understandable tears.

Of course one can take the person to whom one wishes to give the present to the furrier, the jeweler, the leather merchant or the bookseller, but unless you know that person very well the question of money will cloud the motive of the gift. Should you then pretend to be pleased when you feel let down? Have not the slightest doubt about that. If someone wants to give you pleasure you must give them pleasure in return. A white lie is better than a black grief. Above all little children's presents should be enthusiastically accepted. I still cannot remember without a pang an awful day when I was a child. With my tiny savings I had bought one of my sisters a toy ironing board and iron. She did not like them and threw them back in my face. Sixty years later I am still unconsoled. It was too unfair.

"Poor mankind!" once remarked Abbé Mugnier, "Two thousand years and they still haven't invented an eighth deadly sin!"

Nor have they been able to invent many new toys. Motherhood and the household for the girls, war and means of transport for boys are the perennial themes. Of course war changes. Instead of the panoply of the Sioux, bows and arrows, the shop windows are full of the "little Atomic Pilot, complete with automatic bomb release and a village that blows up." That is not progress. But dolls, all honor to them, do not change. As Alain said, it is Woman who saves what Man needs if he is to remain Man. May she help us to give peace to the world. This is my wish for the New Year. A Happy Christmas to you, my dear. *Adieu.*